apartment

apartment

STYLISH SOLUTIONS
FOR APARTMENT LIVING

ALAN POWERS

PHOTOGRAPHY BY CHRIS EVERARD

RYLAND
PETERS
& SMALL

London New York

First published in the United States in 2001
by Ryland Peters & Small Inc.,
519 Broadway
5th Floor
New York
NY 10012

10 9 8 7 6 5 4 3 2 1

ISBN: 1 84172 160 3

Printed in China

Designer Vicky Holmes
Managing Editor Annabel Morgan
Senior Editor Clare Double
Location and Picture Research Manager Kate Brunt
Location Researcher Sarah Hepworth
Picture Researcher Jenny Drane
Production Patricia Harrington
Art Director Gabriella Le Grazie
Publishing Director Alison Starling

Stylist Christina Wilson
Italian Locations Enrica Stabile

www.rylandpeters.com

CONTENTS

INTRODUCTION

Apartment living is the essence of urban existence, allowing people to live close together while providing security, privacy, and comfort within a larger social and architectural scale. The outside of an apartment building is seldom a dramatic piece of architecture, but inside there may be charming original features. In some cases, the apartment is a blank canvas on which it is possible to create a new home with a character of its own.

This book shows a variety of ways in which this has been done, showing that the glamour of loft living has not superseded life in more traditional, purpose-built apartments. Many examples are the homes of architects and designers, who have been able to experiment with new ideas. Nearly all the people whose homes are illustrated here are involved in some form of creative activity, and the illustrations show this not only in their choice of unusual furniture and objects, but in their ability to make day-to-day living into an art form. There are many ideas about choices of furniture and fixtures that are applicable in any household situation.

If there is a design secret that is special to apartments, it is to consider the inherent qualities of a space. Even if a radical transformation is going to happen, there are certain things that cannot be changed; the direction of the light, the floor-to-ceiling height, the overall layout, and the size and direction of the windows. Most apartments have a flat floor running through, so the treatment of the floor is an important design element. It is possible to make spaces seem larger than they really are, and many of the designs in this book show simple ways of doing this with room dividers rather than walls, the use of well-placed mirrors, and the avoidance of small, cramped subdivisions of space. The other secret of increasing the illusion of space is control over the number of one's possessions, and discipline about keeping them neat. Storage is therefore a key issue, and one for which some ingenious and visually attractive solutions can be found in these pages.

The case studies in this book are grouped according to different visual themes, showing what a wide range of successful interior styles is available. None is entirely conventional—it is noticeable that not a single one has curtains, and many even have no window shades—but they all provide for the basic necessities of life: eating, relaxing, sleeping, and entertaining.

Opposite "Mansion flats" like these are found in many areas of London, England. Although they seldom rank as distinguished architecture in their own right, they still provide comfortable apartment spaces with good, high ceilings.

Left A typical European-style apartment building in Italy, modeled on a Renaissance town palace, with one main entrance to a courtyard and a hierarchy of levels above.

Above Twentieth-century apartment buildings have usually been designed to maximize land value. Story heights are equal throughout, and the only "special" space is the penthouse, made possible by steel-frame construction.

THE STORY
OF THE APARTMENT

1850s–1900s

In the cities of continental Europe, most of which were hemmed in by defensive walls and fortifications until the second half of the nineteenth century, apartment living was the norm for people at almost all levels of society, carrying on a practice of living on one floor that had originally developed in the great shared townhouses and palaces of the Middle Ages. In England, living in "chambers," with service provided, was usual only for bachelors. Practicality and respect for family values in the Victorian period meant that private houses were generally favored for couples, although there was still a demand for apartments in London for use during short seasons in the capital, or by those who were prepared to break with convention.

London acquired its first prestige block of "mansion flats" in 1881, when Richard Norman Shaw designed Albert Hall Mansions, overlooking Kensington Gardens. Partly inspired by French ways of planning apartments, it looks more like a row of overgrown Dutch canalside townhouses. Inside, the apartments are an early example of duplex planning, with extra floors of bedrooms at the rear, and tall living rooms lit by narrow sash windows overlooking the park.

In 1884, Whitehall Court, with its ornate château-style skyline, was built overlooking the River Thames, but the Dutch gable style proved more popular over the next thirty years. New York's Dakota building, of the same year, overlooks Central Park at 72nd Street and is more like an enlarged townhouse. It was situated so far uptown that it acquired its nickname from the remote Dakota territory. However, the popularity of this building among artists and bohemians helped to start a fashion for apartment living that has continued in New York ever since, encouraged by high property values in popular neighborhoods.

After 1900, apartment buildings began to develop distinct architectural personalities of their own. Reinforced concrete construction now made it possible not only to build tall, but also to change the shape of buildings. Auguste Perret's block in rue Franklin, Paris (1903–4), broke the street line to give a more varied outlook to each apartment. Around 1909, Henri Sauvage, another French architect with a desire to apply new techniques, developed the idea of a building fronted with terraces that stepped back as they ascended, allowing more light to reach the street and reflect off glazed white tile surfaces.

Opposite above Whitehall Court in London was designed by the architects Archer & Green in a French château style. For many years there were no kitchens in the apartments, and residents had to eat in a dining room on the ground floor. The location suited people who wanted to travel from nearby Charing Cross station, the gateway to continental Europe, where apartments were the normal way of living in cities.

Opposite below left Edward S. Clark, one of the heirs to the Singer sewing machine fortune, commissioned Henry J. Hardenbergh to design an apartment building on the west side of Central Park, New York, at 72nd Street. Built in 1884, it became known as The Dakota.

Opposite below right Apartments by Henry Sauvage in rue Vavin, Paris, 1912. This practical design used the strength of reinforced concrete to create a stepped section, giving each apartment a generous balcony with a reasonable degree of privacy and the maximum amount of sunlight.

Left The conventional classicism of the Third Republic in France was challenged by Auguste Perret's apartment building in rue Franklin, Paris, decorated with low-relief patterns of flowers set in the panels of the concrete frame.

AFTER 1900, APARTMENTS BEGAN TO DEVELOP ARCHITECTURAL PERSONALITIES OF THEIR OWN

1920s–1930s

During the 1920s, architects looked at apartment buildings with a new sense of optimism and opportunity, inspired by ideas of lightweight modern living in a world just beginning to recover from the shock of World War I. They hoped to banish the dirt and grime of old-fashioned cities and enjoy a clean new world of electric technology and sunlight.

The Swiss architect Le Corbusier (1887–1965), who rose to fame at the beginning of the period as the prophet of this new spirit, planned cities that would be composed solely of apartment buildings, bringing open vistas and plenty of sunlight and greenery to their inhabitants. He believed that conventional streets were no longer viable, and that cars should run through downtown areas on specially dedicated freeways, separated from pedestrians, who could enjoy strolling through parkland instead. This vision was deliberately inimical to the crowded intimacy that is now valued in urban living.

When Le Corbusier visited London in 1935, he was impressed by the Highpoint "flats," the work of Russian architect Berthold Lubetkin (1901–90). Highpoint's construction was entirely of concrete, finished in dazzling white paint with jaunty balconies and long windows, which could be folded completely back, in the living rooms. A handful of similar buildings were built in London, aiming to combine convenience of internal planning with the excitement of an architectural vision of the future. The technical resources of

DURING THE 1920s, ARCHITECTS LOOKED AT APARTMENTS WITH A NEW SENSE OF OPTIMISM

Above Giuseppe Terragni and Pietro Lingeri's Villa Rustici apartments in Milan make striking use of a white-painted concrete grid that contrasts with the earth colors of the main walls. In addition to providing a novel form of garden terrace, the open front wall allows apartments at the rear to see onto the street.

Left One of Le Corbusier's first apartment blocks, the Maison Clarté of 1930, is sited in a typical urban quarter of Geneva. It was commissioned by a steel contractor as a speculative development and therefore was particularly well constructed. Its combination of high technology and traditional urbanism represents a mixture with which contemporary architects and apartment dwellers feel most comfortable, even though Le Corbusier wanted to erase the conventional city.

Right The penthouse at Highpoint II, London (see pages 84–89), was designed by Berthold Lubetkin, architect of the two adjacent buildings, for himself. Influenced by Le Corbusier's own rooftop apartment in Paris, Lubetkin introduced curved shapes into the roof in contrast to the straight lines of the main building.

MODERN ARCHITECTURE IN THE 1930s MEANT DIFFERENT THINGS TO DIFFERENT PEOPLE

Above These apartment buildings lined up alongside Park Avenue in New York, and dating from the interwar years, gradually grew taller and taller in an effort to get the best value from their sites. Their stepped tops, many housing luxurious penthouse suites, give them the look of ziggurats from the ancient world.

Left The interior of a spectacular 1930 Art Deco apartment in London created by the American-born architect Howard Robertson, who later designed the Shell Center in London. The emphasis on geometric shapes, decorative rugs, and sleek and streamlined built-in furniture and fixtures is typical of the period. It feels like the ideal location for a sophisticated Manhattan cocktail party.

Right With their dominantly horizontal windows and distinct resemblance to an ocean-going liner, the Shangri-La apartments on Ocean Boulevard in Santa Monica, California, were designed by the American architect William E. Foster between 1939 and 1940. The building has a streamlined design and an evocative Hollywood-style name, in a trend that went out of date after World War II, but has long been back in fashion.

modern building were capable of turning into poetry in the hands of sufficiently inspired architects like Le Corbusier and Lubetkin. Giuseppe Terragni (1906–43) and Pietro Lingeri (1894–1968) achieved a gentle form of fantasy at the Villa Rustici (1933–35), an apartment building in an inner suburb of Milan (illustrated on page 12). Terragni bridged across between the wings, allowing light to penetrate to the back of the building and giving the apartments at the front the use of a terraced garden, supported on the thinnest of concrete slabs.

Modern architecture in the 1930s meant different things to different people. Faithful followers of Le Corbusier and the other modern "masters" were aware of a need to remain faithful to an ideal that combined a consistency of construction (preferably in modern materials such as concrete or steel) with a vision of a changing society. When designing apartments, they were seldom doing something as simple as giving clients what they wanted. These architects wanted to use their buildings as models of a better world in the future.

There was a range of alternative positions during these years. Tudor City in New York (1925–28), with its halftimbered architectural detail concentrated near the skyline, is a landmark near the United Nations headquarters. New York also has a large number of classical and Colonial apartment buildings, with regular grids of wooden sash windows set across large faces of brickwork. Steel-frame construction not only allowed for additional height, but also facilitated the building of stepped-back terraces above the height limit for the street. Unlike Henri Sauvage's stepped sections, these were a kind of addition atop the main building, providing valuable penthouse suites with the best views of the city. In London the valuable sites overlooking Park Lane and Hyde Park were rebuilt as apartments between the wars, with the great English classicist, Sir Edwin Lutyens, acting as consultant. His rooftop pavilions peep over the trees.

In these "period"-style buildings, the entrance lobby and communal spaces were usually designed in the same style, and the apartments themselves might have molding and fireplaces or other architectural details to match, but it was quite possible for owners to customize the interiors, using their own decorators and designers, as they still do today. Howard Robertson's 1930s apartment is a good example. It was located in Portman Court, a fashionable building in a classical style in one of London's most stylish Georgian squares. The interior, however, is pure Art Deco, taking its inspiration from examples of modernism that had filtered down from their original sources and become a versatile but essentially decorative language, celebrated in the Paris international exhibition of 1925.

Art Deco and modernism are easily confused, as they often resemble each other and ran side by side through the same period. William E. Foster's Shangri-La apartments in Santa Monica can be categorized as Art Deco because, although there is hardly any "applied decoration" as such, they represent the adoption of a modern image for a building that is essentially conventional and conservative in its composition and construction, as delightful and appropriate as it is in its seaside setting among the palm trees.

AFTER THE WAR, NEW REGULATIONS MEANT THAT A GENERALLY LIGHTER LOOK BECAME POSSIBLE

1940s–1950s AND BEYOND

After World War II, apartment buildings continued to compete with private houses in Britain and North America. As car ownership grew, parking, usually in an underground garage, became desirable. It was also important to make sure that buildings looked conspicuously different from prewar examples. Architecturally, this was achieved in several ways. Before the war, many of the construction methods that architects wished to adopt were prohibited by building laws that were slow to move with the times and acknowledge new building techniques. After the war, new regulations meant that a generally lighter look became possible, with larger areas of glass and a clearer distinction between the load-bearing frame of a building and its infill of windows or opaque panels.

The most dramatic demonstration of a new type of apartment was the twin towers by Mies van der Rohe at 860–880 South Lake Shore Drive, Chicago, built between 1949 and 1951. Mies had come to the U.S. in 1938, and refined his style to acknowledge Chicago's steel-frame building tradition. At Lake Shore Drive, he produced an economical design of exceptional elegance, rising sheer from the ground with an inset lobby at the base. Each bay of four tall windows between the main load-bearing steel verticals was treated with similar vertical steel sections, which were in fact only a form of architectural decoration welded onto the face of the building. With floor-to-ceiling windows, each with white curtains to maintain uniformity, the new buildings in Chicago were to become the model for Mies's Seagram office building in New York and many other corporate skyscrapers.

On a visit to Chicago in 1954, British architect Sir Denys Lasdun visited the Lake Shore Drive apartments and was impressed by the consistency and discipline of their design. Having previously designed some notable examples of public housing, Lasdun received the commission for 26 St. James's Place in London (1958), where a new luxury apartment building was inserted into a historic line of buildings facing Green Park. Lasdun's strong horizontals of white concrete contributed a classical serenity.

A unique architectural form appeared in Chicago with Bertrand Goldberg's Marina City, 1959–63. Goldberg was an apprentice in Mies van der Rohe's office, and Marina City profits from the lessons about the application of

Opposite above left An interior converted by Higgins and Ney in 1954 in a prewar apartment building shows the typical 1950s "flashgap" style, with the hearth and fire hood appearing to hover in space. Simple furniture is given a few folksy Mediterranean touches.

Opposite above right Mies van der Rohe's famous apartment blocks in Lake Shore Drive, Chicago, invented a new style for tall buildings throughout the world. Although the buildings are standard in form, the relationship between the two masses is carefully considered in relation to the setting.

Opposite below A suave newcomer in St. James's, London, Sir Denys Lasdun's apartments at 26 St. James's Place are a model of how to place a new building in an historic context. Each unit has a high-ceilinged living space to the front, with lower bedrooms to the rear—not dissimilar to Richard Norman Shaw's scheme at Albert Hall Mansions.

Left Looking like fantasies of science fiction, Bertrand Goldberg's Marina City apartment blocks in Chicago radiate from a central core of lifts and services, with apartments arranged "like flower petals."

industrial building techniques that he learned there and even earlier as a student at the famous Bauhaus school in his native Germany. The twin towers, known as the Corn Cobs, rise from the banks of the Chicago River, with parking ramps on the lower levels and a marina giving direct access to the water.

Apartment buildings come in many different shapes and sizes. Perhaps the most commonly held image is that of Le Corbusier's Unité d'Habitation at Marseille, France, a typical "slab" of a kind favored for public housing all over the world. The building was conceived at the end of World War II in 1945 and completed in 1951. It was the fulfillment of Le Corbusier's dream, for he had spent most of his life imagining possible forms of communal living, drawing his initial inspiration from the peaceful cells of a Carthusian monastery near Florence. He imagined the Unité to be like an ocean liner, where all the needs of life are taken care of, so it has sports facilities, a shopping street, and a nursery school on the roof. Even ice was made on site and delivered to each resident. The individual apartments have a double-height living room connected to a balcony that spans the width of the building.

Le Corbusier's idea of modern living amid greenery and away from busy roads was also achieved in Eric Lyons's Span Estates in Britain, built in the 1950s and 1960s. These apartment buildings were not massive slabs or huge towers, but three storys high at most. The individual apartments were not large, but planned to make best use of the space, with wide windows giving a double aspect. There was no intention to create great works of architecture, but rather to produce a modern equivalent of the rowhouses of Georgian London, which married the social needs with the building technology of the time. What makes Span Estates special is the landscaping, comprising not only attractive planting and grass, but also a sense of composed space between the buildings to create enclosure and security without claustrophobia. The journey from the parking area to the front door usually includes a series of glimpses under and through the buildings, and the open spaces were intended to be used like the shared garden squares of London.

Hans Scharoun, an architect of the same generation as Le Corbusier and Mies van der Rohe, felt that modern architecture should offer a liberation from the exact forms of a geometric grid. He nicknamed the twin apartment buildings he built to the north of Stuttgart, Germany (1954–59) "Romeo and Juliet," since he felt they were essentially a male–female pair. Romeo is eighteen storys high, with each apartment different in plan, and few right-angled corners. Juliet is an eight-story horseshoe. The apartments have balconies swinging off the corners, screened for privacy and against wind.

Lake Shore Drive, the Unité d'Habitation, and Romeo and Juliet offer three different views on what is important in life, each with persuasive advocates. Nowadays, we may accept that there is no right answer, but that was far from the case in the 1960s, when construction of public housing was at a peak and the emphasis was on standardization. Romeo and Juliet would then have been considered eccentric outsiders, but today, architects and residents might well prefer this expression of individualism.

Above left The Priory, Blackheath, London, completed in 1956, is a typical example of a low-rise Span development. The architect was Eric Lyons.

Above right Hans Scharoun's Romeo and Juliet apartments in Stuttgart were designed to fit the needs of a particular site, while allowing a sense of individuality, expressed through plan, form, and color, to show.

Below left The exterior of Le Corbusier's Unité d'Habitation, Marseille. The application of a variety of colors to the side faces of the balconies was intended to individualize the apartments within the "liner" of the whole structure. The blank band reveals the position of the internal shopping street.

Below right A crèche in the Unité d'Habitation. This view shows the double-height space opening out into the balcony from above. Built-in furniture helps to keep the spaces clear. Women's and children's needs were uppermost in Le Corbusier's mind when he was designing this famous building.

THE UNITÉ D'HABITATION WAS THE FULFILLMENT OF LE CORBUSIER'S DREAM

APARTMENT PROFILES

CONTEMPORARY SIMPLICITY

LIGHT CREATING SPACE
HIGH MODERN COOL

High above the traffic in one of the most select areas of Manhattan, the architect Michael Gabellini has created a strongly unified set of spaces using richly restrained materials, and incorporating a variety of furniture he designed especially for this home. The apartment was especially remodeled to display an outstanding photography collection, ranging from Fox Talbot to the present day, and its subtle coloring allows the historic black-and-white prints to glow with their own interior light. The apartment is a lower penthouse and has three aspects, to north, west, and south, with two roof terraces, so it enjoys an abundance of natural light.

Left A gateway frames the entrance to this austerely luxurious penthouse from a hallway behind the dark wood screen wall. The sitting area brings the dominant line of the space close to the stone floor. The slender support for the bench seat helps to emphasize the smooth curve of its profile.

Above A collection of classic early photographs adds interest to the living room without detracting from the decorative unity. The Indian stone sculpture introduces a calm physical presence.

Left The dining area mixes materials in a creative way, with a magnificent stone table offset by the rustic lightness of the chairs. The table top, of limestone from upstate New York, was carefully selected to be as far as possible without grain or figure. Nature does not always deal in perfection, however, and the owner has come to enjoy the subtle coloration that runs across the surface. A stainless-steel shelf in the foreground echoes the kitchen appliances beyond. This end of the apartment is hung with the more recent examples of photography in the collection. Double-aspect lighting at the corner of the apartment animates the space.

Right Japanese woven rush pillows and sandals add to the rich cultural mixture of the main bedroom, where the bed appears to hover in space. Controls for lighting are set on a panel concealed beneath it. The Greek stool at the foot of the bed adds a touch of warmth and color. The profile of the ceiling has received as much attention as the other areas, making a "room within a room" over the bed.

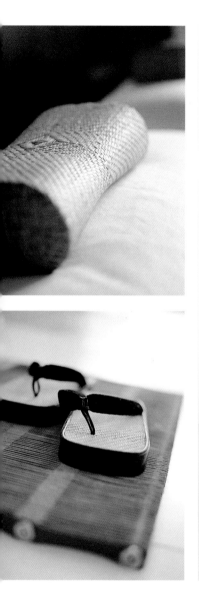

The apartment's plan includes an ingenious series of movable partitions that can be configured to create a separate guest suite, while leaving a free flow of space for every day. In a more intimate sitting area, a large contemporary photograph is mounted on a sliding section of wall that rolls back to reveal a television set.

The floor, composed of pale honey-colored yard-square stones, is the unifying design element, running throughout the apartment and providing a dimensional grid. The remainder of the palette materials are disciplined, but not monotonous. A wall of dark wood delineates two solid blocks of storage space with concealed doors, as well as the area behind the bed in the master bedroom. Stainless steel features in the kitchen and in the coffee table in the main sitting area. The glass partitions between the two bathrooms and their adjoining bedrooms turn from transparent to opaque at the flick of a

switch, due to a special lighting device acting within the glass.

The seating is restrained, but its velvety texture and mixture of three colors adds a degree of richness. The bench seat is by Michael Gabellini, and the tub chairs were copied, by arrangement, from some that the apartment owner admired in Tokyo. Around the limestone dining table, set dynamically off-center on its stone support, sit Danish wooden chairs with rope seats, adding an element of tactile pleasure to what might have been too austere a setting for food. A set of two square stools and a long stool in the bedroom, wooden with woven leather seats, was made in Greece. These pieces have a timeless classical elegance that complements the photograph of a nude torso displayed over the bed, and introduce a quality of handcraftsmanship into a deliberately industrial aesthetic.

At the turn of the nineteenth century, Frank Lloyd Wright declared that the machine was an ally of natural materials, revealing their surfaces without human intervention. The developing aesthetic of photography, in which nature's integrity was preserved by a device that revealed new wonders from the existing world, was similar. Minimalism in architecture and design continues in this line, reducing the range of possibilities to intensify the experience, and this apartment, whose identity is influenced by photographic history, prompts similar reflections. It allows nature to mediate between man and machine through the revealed grain of materials.

Above There is a world of reflections in this corner of the bathroom, where the Carrara marble sink and the cloudy glass of the partitions meet mirror and the stainless steel of the faucet and supporting frame. This encounter is surrealistically monitored by an orchid.

Left The apartment is linked by a spine passageway, where sliding partitions allow privacy when it is wanted. This picture shows how the unity of space has been preserved and the structural columns, like the one in the foreground, used creatively to modulate the space. The bathtub, a corner of which is in view, was carved from a solid piece of Carrara marble, specially chosen at the quarry in Italy, and entered the apartment by crane one blustery February weekend.

DESIGNED TO REVEAL THE CHARACTER OF A PALETTE OF LUXURIOUS MATERIALS, THIS APARTMENT MAKES INGENIOUS USE OF SPACE AS A BACKGROUND TO CONTEMPORARY LIVING IN TIMELESS PERFECTION

Left With no curtains or floor coverings, space and light become the main ingredients in this Parisian apartment, but the variety among the furniture and decorative objects makes it a very personal statement of minimalist principles.

Right above Storage is built into a cavity in the wall, and the effect is cleverly doubled by the framed mirror. Paintings propped on the floor bring the eye down to ground level—always a good way to enhance the feeling of space.

Right below The floor lamp with its square shade has an individuality that is shared by all the objects in the apartment.

FRENCH POLISH
A CONTEMPORARY MIX

The minimalist way of designing interiors is often misunderstood. If modernism is taken to be a style that is already stripped down and bereft of period references, then minimalism takes on the role of ultra-modern, in the sense that everything is even more detached from references of time and place. This does not necessarily have to be so. Minimalism can also be a form of classicism, in the sense of cutting away superfluous details in order to discover the essence. The essence of what? Of a city, an apartment, an individual, combined in a clearly stated ideal of living. This Paris apartment inspires such thoughts. It is also unmistakably French, with its cast-iron balconies appearing like the background of a Matisse or Dufy painting.

The rooms suggest an artist's studio, where accidents of the existing character are allowed to remain, not only to save the labor of removing them, but also to help in modulating the space and light, which are the chief elements with which the modernist designer works.

Surfaces are especially important in minimalism, adding a sensual element often lacking from purely industrial interiors. As many people moving into old buildings have discovered, old floorboards and wall plaster are better at providing a rich but unobtrusive quality of texture and color than any modern building materials. In this case, the marble fireplace adds an element of opulence, affirming a French tradition dating from the seventeenth century that the fireplace should always be the richest and most dominating part of any room. It acts as a unit with its overmantel mirror, which in those times would have been a conspicuous token of wealth. Another mirror is used more subtly and

Left The partition wall helps to enclose the dining area and provide spatial variety. This view emphasizes the importance of an interesting floor surface, while the glazed door not only admits borrowed light into the passageway, but acts as a source of reflections in the room. The marble fireplace is one of the elements that make this an unmistakably French apartment; traditionally the fireplace dominated any French room.

Above left With its industrial-style equipment, the corner sink has a professional look to it, while the elegant swan-neck of the water faucet adds an element of fantasy.

Above right At first view, there is nothing special about the kitchen, but it has a unity of color scheme and a choice selection of objects that seems just right in context. The whole suggests that food is meant to be enjoyed rather than aestheticized.

surprisingly in the corner of the room, to double the seemingly random pattern of small storage cupboards, reflecting a view into those whose doors are half-open toward the room.

A further example of ingenious storage, essential to the preservation of the minimalist mirage, can be found in the bedroom units, which have space in their wide doors for racks of small items. The bathroom, too, has an intriguing pattern of hinged flaps in the wall, recalling the thick walls of old farmhouses that provided space for the earliest cupboards.

The furniture in this apartment mixes old and new in a relaxed way. There is a unity of warm dark coloring in wood and fabrics, but there is also a lively contrast between the "modern classic" Arne Jacobsen dining chairs, with their refined, lightweight forms, set under a table with the same steel and wood aesthetic, and the monumentality of the closet

BANKS OF CUNNING STORAGE SPACES OPEN UNEXPECTEDLY AND IN COMPLEX PATTERNS. THEY ARE UNEXPECTED BUT HAVE A CHARMING PRACTICALITY

Above An ingenious way of using the height of the room for storage without needing to climb up to find things: shirts on hangers drop down out of the closet for easy access. The insides of the doors are built like boxes to give additional storage.
Left Storage units have been built out from the wall with an architectural boldness that also makes them a practical way of storing clothes for convenient access. Strongly figured unpainted plywood matches the quality of "found" materials that runs through the whole apartment. The rococo fireplace and bold overmantel mirror are a variation on the theme established in the main living space.

Right A symphony in steel and driftwood: the bathroom blurs the line between practicality and decoration still further, yet preserves a visual clarity throughout. The effect of the different angles of cupboard doors echoes that in the main living space.

Below While the many hinged frames on this heated towel rack may not be strictly necessary, they demonstrate a further episode in the enjoyment of sliding and turning gadgets that runs through the other functional areas. The handsome nuts that join the pipes, with the shadows cast on the wall behind, create a rhythmic background.

between the windows. The armchair, reminiscent of the primitive modernism of Gerrit Rietveld in the 1920s, contrasts with the comfort of the chaise longue.

The kitchen shows how standard units can enhance the anticipation of good food, while a "designer" kitchen can seem too perfect to cook in. The narrow hanging rack on the wall also acts as a display shelf where practical equipment and decorative found objects can exist side by side. The chopping board can slide across the pressed steel sink in the inset grooves, beneath the eye of the amazing swan-necked waterspout.

This simple one-bedroom apartment has the kind of effortless elegance that has always been associated with French style, and which would still be present even if the markers of French identity were not. It is a kind of design language that can use anything it finds, not requiring a complete clear-out to make things new. Perhaps it accompanies a certain laconic economy of effort in the French language itself, where the classical roots of words give them resonances beyond their dictionary definitions.

THE SIXTIES BOUNCE BACK
COMPACT CLARITY

The Barbican Centre in the City of London, begun during the 1960s, is a place that tends to divide opinion sharply. Outsiders often find it difficult to navigate through and around the tall residential towers and rows of apartments that form a series of terraces and walkways overlooking areas of garden and lake. For residents, however, it offers the convenience of living right in the middle of London with many local facilities, including a theater, cinema, concert hall, and exhibition gallery. These aspects particularly appealed to a Belgian couple seeking a London base. They were fortunate enough to find a penthouse apartment in one of the lower buildings, with a barrel-vaulted concrete roof that lifts the space and allows a direct view of the dome of St. Paul's Cathedral. The apartment had been rented for many years, and although some of the original features were unaltered it needed a careful refit to meet the needs of the new owners.

Opposite This Barbican apartment is simply and appropriately furnished, recreating the mood of the original late 1960s period. The buildings in this large complex have an ancient-Roman quality of robustness in their materials and detailing, a value evident here. The projecting strip of wood at the junction of the wall and vault conceals miniature strip lighting that throws light upward onto the curve of the roof.

Left The apartment's new owners have inserted a mezzanine level to create a bed platform, accessed by these steep cantilevered steps. The slits in the underside of the platform provide ventilation for the bed base overhead.

Right The furnishings chosen are deliberately sparse in order not to clutter the space. These Eames chairs are lightweight and comfortable.

A STRONG ARCHITECTURAL STATEMENT HAS BEEN HARMONIOUSLY AMPLIFIED, ADDING EXTRA SPACE IN THE SPIRIT OF THE ORIGINAL

FINE DETAILING AND CAREFUL FURNISHING RECREATE THE SPIRIT OF THE SIXTIES IN STYLE

The owners already knew architect Joe Hagan of USE Architects. His refit of this relatively small apartment is both elegant and practical.

The apartment is a long rectangle in plan, with windows at each end. The stairway arrives at the midpoint of one side, giving access to a narrow passage that almost immediately introduces you into the main room. Here the height and the curve of the roof can be enjoyed, with a wonderful quality of light bouncing off the white walls and a view made up mostly of sky. Wood-framed windows give access to a wide, south-facing balcony. One wall has been papered in Japanese grass-cloth, giving a warmth of texture and tone that is authentic to the period of the building. A small work desk is built into a recess in the side wall. The kitchen lies behind the back wall, accessed via flush-fitting double doors. The owners wanted to keep the original steel sink, which has been cleaned up, but they have added a new counter on the opposite wall. The kitchen has skylight windows only, but they offer a glimpse of sky through an arched opening in the concrete wall outside.

The bathroom, also with most of its original features, and whose subtlety of design is a delight to the present owners, backs onto the kitchen. This leaves the bedroom space at the rear of the apartment, where Joe Hagan has made the greatest changes. Instead of having a rather crowded conventional bedroom with a traditional bed, a mezzanine platform has been inserted, reached by a steep flight of wooden steps that are a sculptural feature in their own right. The bed is a simple mattress on the floor, with concealed lighting panels at the head and foot and a low guard rail where the platform meets the ladder stair. The study space

Far left The new bed platform has created a useful workspace on the lower level of the former bedroom, and this has been elegantly equipped with roomy shelves and storage drawers, plus a small desk.

Left The narrow hall is filled with borrowed light from the stairwell and allows room for spare furniture.

Right The bed platform is reached by a wooden ladder stair, neatly slotted in against the side of a new closet space. Up above, it makes a delightful sleeping area, light and airy, with a feeling of being close to the sky. Underneath, a sleek and understated desk teamed with an Eames Aluminum Group chair leaves plenty of free floor space.

beneath benefits from a view of the full height of the room. Sheltered underneath the mezzanine is a practical storage unit, neatly detailed in a style that is convincingly appropriate to that of the apartment. The simple device of moving the original glazed panel beside the door a couple of feet into the hallway has made the new space both larger and more interesting.

In the hall, two windows open onto the brightly lit top of the stairwell, giving borrowed light to what would otherwise be the dark central zone of the apartment. Many Barbican residents screen these windows, but here there is little need for concealment, and the original intention of the building's architects is not interfered with.

The Eames Aluminum chairs and Saarinen Tulip dining set, all appropriate to the style and period of the apartment, already belonged to the owners, whose hometown is the European manufacturing center for Knoll International, original makers of these pieces.

THE KITCHEN AND BATHROOM, BOTH LIT FROM HIGH WINDOWS, ARE SECRET SPACES WHERE MANY ORIGINAL FEATURES HAVE BEEN PRESERVED

Left This view shows the relationship between the kitchen and the main living room, with the hallway to one side, enclosed by a lowered ceiling. The double doors allow the kitchen to be incorporated into the living room or shut away completely as required. The dining table is a version of Eero Saarinen's classic design with a teak top.

Above The principal kitchen fixtures have been lovingly preserved, including the recessed stove on the rear wall with its high-level knobs and the stainless-steel sink. An elegant row of glass-fronted storage cabinets has been added by the new owners in an appropriate style to complement the original fixtures.

Right The top-lit bathroom is a miniature version of the monumentality of the Barbican, with a sink solidly built into a concrete tiled top. The mirrors and towel rods are all original fixtures, including a medicine cabinet and a small mirror panel on the side wall, which creates an all-round view and increases the sense of light and space in this room.

DESIGN IDEAS OF THE 1970s GAIN A FRESH IRONIC TWIST IN A COORDINATED SCHEME

Left This corner of the living room looks almost like a throwback to the early 1970s, with the LP albums in their round-cornered storage unit, but in fact all the furniture in this view was designed specially for the apartment in the late 1990s, including the abstract artwork on the wall, made with colored-laminate panels.

Right The rounded corners of the Eero Saarinen dining table were the original inspiration for the distinctive style of the apartment.

Below The colors on the doors of this cabinet combine with those in the artwork over it to make a sequence that extends into the green and yellow wall colors to be seen in the rooms beyond; a three-dimensional color composition in space.

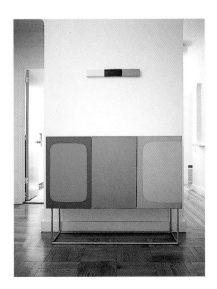

COLOR COCKTAIL
THE ART OF LIVING

New York apartments are always a surprise. The exterior of the building gives no premonition of what you are going to find inside, and then the personality of the owner may be refracted through that of the designer. This small one-bedroom apartment, in a 1930s building in New York's Chelsea, is very much a personal statement by the designer Lloyd Schwan, containing many pieces and artworks designed by him.

Freestanding as well as built-in pieces in this apartment are Lloyd Schwan's work. Even the works of art on the walls are by him, chosen to build up the subtle effect of color relationships and sequences.

Schwan says that his basic principle was to keep everything open, to take advantage of the features that were already there, and, most of all, to enable the owner to be neat. Most of the furniture that is not seating is storage, and comes in an attractive series of forms that have their own sculptural quality.

The general look of the apartment is reminiscent of the late 1960s or early 1970s, based on the lamps, the Saarinen tables, and the Jacobsen chairs—some of the few items not designed by Schwan. These pieces all have simple curved outlines, and Schwan's storage boxes, with their rounded corners, echo this feeling, as do the vases displayed inside them, the chest units and even the bed's headboard.

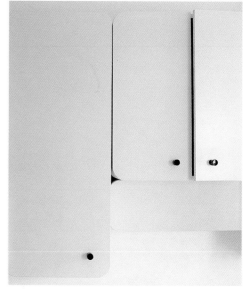

A KNOWING AWARENESS OF HARMONY AND CONTRAST GIVES EVERY FEATURE AN ADDED SIGNIFICANCE, PRODUCING AN AMPLIFICATION OF THE EVERYDAY THAT TYPIFIES THE 1990s

Far left Delicious colors for dinner: the wide opening between the dining area and the kitchen reveals an array of mint-green storage cupboards, arranged with the artful casualness so characteristic of Lloyd Schwan's design work.

Left There is a graceful ease about the way these units of different sizes are assembled. The void spaces where their curved corners meet continues the design language of the apartment and gives each its individuality.

Right In other hands, this sideboard could simply have had four equal doors, but by introducing a narrow extra strip at the left-hand end, Lloyd Schwan has pushed it off-center and given the piece a dynamic quality. The cluster of carefully placed still-life objects, reminiscent of a Giorgio Morandi painting, is an important aspect of the composition in color and form. Arne Jacobsen "Ant" chairs echo the curves of the bottles and emphasize the period look.

Above "Without enough storage, you're doomed," believes Lloyd Schwan. His set of bedroom pieces makes storage a positive part of the room's character, with carefully considered relationships between the separate parts. The bedside table has a distinctive personality of its own; it is paired with one in different colors.

Right The white wall-mounted units in the bedroom achieve a kind of orchestration from their different but related forms. The main storage contrasts this playfulness with a regular grid of square-cornered doors, forming a substantial volume of space in the place occupied formerly by the closet.

Opposite above The light checked material of the bed linen and the warm neutrality of the carpet add a controlled but domestic touch, without which many modern apartments tend to feel sterile and chilly. Colors for accessories also need to be carefully considered.

Opposite below A classic modern lamp and an "Ant" chair by Arne Jacobsen set the scene for this attractive study corner in the bedroom. Lloyd Schwan's distinctive color-laminate artwork ties the visual composition together.

CAREFULLY CHOSEN TEXTILES SOFTEN THE DOMINANT VOCABULARY OF
COLORED LAMINATES, WHICH PLAY SUBTLE GAMES TO DISTURB THE
EXPECTATION OF SUGAR-SWEET PRETTINESS THEY INITIALLY SUGGEST

In terms of their construction, these pieces work well with the laminates that are the basis of Lloyd
Schwan's games with color. These relate to individual pieces of furniture, like the three-drawer striped
bedside chest and the sideboard, with its vertical divisions and two-color panel, but the color is
constructed as a pattern leading the eye from one point to another, up the wall to the artworks and
through the spaces where colors can be seen in conjunction. All is not intended to be harmonious. The
sideboard, in Schwan's words, includes "colors you wouldn't call pretty," and there is a deliberate
desire to create a tension through the colors that will add a dimension of meaning. The same secret
desire for controlled disorder is revealed in the specially made seating, consisting of a loveseat and
two ottomans, which are "conceived as a car accident," although fortunately this subliminal message
is not too strongly pushed home.

FORMAL ELEGANCE

Left Warm light floods uninterrupted into the main sitting area of this Milan apartment designed by Daniela Micol Wajskol. The upholstered comfort offers an invitation to lounge, but the crisp discipline of the decor also requires that you keep your wits about you. The black columns symmetrically positioned on each side of the fireplace are hi-fi speakers. This space leads out of the entrance hall shown on the previous two pages.

Right The yellow Siena marble of the outer fireplace surround sets the gold-colored theme for the room, but the straight lines of this piece and its lack of carving work to establish a timeless architectural formality.

STRUCTURED SIMPLICITY
CITY AND COUNTRY JOINED

To associate the quality of formal elegance with the past would not exactly be wrong, but it is not quite as simple as that. Formality changes its meaning in relation to its context, whether this is a context of manners and behavior, or the physical context of a particular living space. Formality provides a structure against which the fluidity of real life can achieve freedom, rather than imposing restrictions on it. Perhaps this is where elegance comes in, if one understands it to mean a pleasurable and economical adjustment of means to ends. This apartment in Milan, designed by Daniela Micol Wajskol, combines late eighteenth-century neoclassicism—a legacy of Milan's Napoleonic conquest—with urban and rural influences, to create a modern family home.

A RESTRAINED BACKGROUND ALLOWS A FEW TOUCHES OF COLORED SPARKLE TO ADD VITALITY WITHOUT DOMINATING THE SPACE

The formal elegance of the apartment is based on certain ground rules. The color palette is deliberately restrained and is largely limited to a range between white and brown, providing the main spaces with a disciplined unity and creating a stage on which the colored clothes of the inhabitants can attract the attention they deserve.

The main sitting area is based on an axial symmetry encouraged by the central fireplace and the flanking frames that enclose the pictures to either side. As vintage architectural drawings, these pictures contribute to the subdued coloring and affirm a link to the past through formal classical design. The simple moldings on the wall, suggesting closed-up doorways, help to establish the scale of the space and repeat the emphasis on framing in the design of the fire surround, creating a recognizably English effect. Everything in the space is kept deliberately low to create a sense of repose.

The objects on the mantelpiece also play their part, adding a little informality and a more modern character just where it is needed, in the form of paired lamps and the conjunction of an abstract sculpture with the enigmatic egg shape in the central frame, acting as an ironic commentary on the whole idea of a symmetrical buildup to the center. The choice of a daybed in the position facing the fireplace helps to

Far left A felicitous visual echo in this corner links the swan-neck of the floor lamp to the curved back of this daybed, a piece equally suitable for solitude or companionship.

Left center This detail of the dining room shows the abundance of light, caught in the clear-glass candlestick and seen through the country simplicity of the flower arrangement.

Left The set of dining chairs, with their delicate cane back panels, embodies the idea of formal elegance in a room where a degree of informality provides a contrast with the other spaces.

Below The deep recesses of the screen wall between the rooms provide useful spaces for extra dining chairs. These French-style chairs with their pink upholstery, a sweet touch in an otherwise sugar-free room, seem like a dessert waiting on the sideboard to be served.

Left The main bedroom offers repose without frills, demonstrating the unity of color and detailing that runs through the whole apartment. The relationship between the tall rectangles of the Empire escritoire and the window is especially satisfying.

Below In the children's bedroom, a pair of antique French beds look their best against the relatively bare walls, leaving plenty of play space for teddy bears and other toys.

BEDROOMS ARE FULL OF LIGHT, WITH A FEW SELECTED PIECES TO STIR IMAGINATION WITH MEMORIES OF THE PAST. FORMAL PIECES MIX COMFORTABLY WITH RUSTIC ELEMENTS

Above A group of potted *Phalaenopsis* orchids, with their fragile petals and slender stems, lighten the mood on the broad marble windowsill.

Left The dark tone of the blue mosaic in the bathroom comes as a surprise after the lightness of the other rooms, but it sets off the polished floors and classic white bathroom fixtures admirably.

establish a strong sight line between the living room and dining room, where the back of an ordinary sofa would interrupt the strength of the axial symmetry by concealing the lower part of the fireplace. As in traditional Italian living, and many contemporary modernist apartments, the comfort of floor coverings is sacrificed to the visual unity that stems from a single flooring material running through a space, reflecting the light from the tall windows.

This sitting space is screened on two sides and opens onto a dining room and a large entrance foyer, where a bold classically patterned rug, in dark blue and gold, warms the stone floor. The dining room is divided from the sitting area by internal windows and glazed doors, creating a sense of movement from indoors to outdoors. Inside the dining room, there is the

Left Warm French gray is a dependable color that responds to the warm brown of the chair backs around the kitchen table and the baskets atop the big hutch. The unfussy character of this piece, with its chicken-wire door panels, contributes to the restrained rustic feeling of the room, and the white china stored inside makes a pleasing catalog of different shapes.

Right The kitchen is practical yet displays plenty of style, especially in the quirky painted table with its piecrust edging and patina of age and usage. This is the sort of piece that can give personality to a whole room. The folding chairs increase the outdoor country feeling.

feeling of sitting on a veranda, flooded with light. In this uncluttered space, the pink toile de Jouy upholstery on the backs of the chairs standing in the recesses of the screen wall makes a pleasing contrast with the solid fabrics chosen elsewhere.

The less formal areas of the apartment are designed with the same restraint, tempered by individual touches that allow each piece of furniture to have its say in the conversation. This is a family apartment, and the children's bedroom introduces a little fantasy in the form of high French-style beds. The main bedroom is more modern in its furnishings, although the Empire escritoire chimes agreeably with the framed rendering of a classical order hung over the head of the bed. In this room, as in many others, the basic proportions of the window openings, coming down to the floor and helping to flood the interior with light, are a major contributor to the feeling of graceful comfort.

The bathroom makes a strong color contrast to the neutral restraint of the other rooms. Its strong cobalt blue emerges from a glittering range of color variations in each of the mosaic tesserae. The pair of old-fashioned pedestal washbasins are sturdy and practical—ceramic classics in their own right.

The use of folding garden chairs and a rough country table with chipped paintwork in the kitchen extends the outdoors feeling and contrasts with the formal mood evident in the dining room. The big hutch set against the side wall in the kitchen is an ideal showcase for the white tableware, setting off its timeless curving shapes, which derive from ancient Greece and Rome and have never been out of fashion since their late eighteenth-century revival. The wicker baskets stacked on top contribute an element of rusticity and another level of formal contrast. The simple design of the kitchen units forms a suitably neutral background for these details.

THE KITCHEN EVOKES A RUSTIC LIFESTYLE, AND ACKNOWLEDGES ITS ROLE IN THE FAMILY HOME, IN PLEASING CONTRAST TO THE MAIN LIVING SPACES

WARMTH AND WIT
STAGE SET FOR A SALON

Some contemporary writers might make one suppose that modernism in home decoration is a compulsory school uniform for anyone aspiring to graduate in cool. But in such a personal aspect of life as decoration, even good things lose their appeal when they are enforced like dress codes. Here, the "right" style is less important than enjoyment.

In the 1980s, when modernism was in partial eclipse, a new, loosely structured eclecticism became popular. A reaction against a science-fiction future that never seemed to arrive, in a world that wanted to remember good things from older times, it was a continuation of 1960s hippy bohemianism, combined with the "Bloomsbury" style of cultural self-assurance that was more dependent on a richly stocked mind than

Above Round tables are a recurrent theme throughout the apartment. In this hall, a fine wooden architectural model sets the tone for the classical character of much of the furnishing. Simple *trompe l'oeil* painting on the walls enlivens the space, and the dramatic light fixture adds a final decorative flourish.

Left A burst of light from unusual corner windows reveals a rich assortment of colors and textures.

on a full bank account. It was anti-consumerist, reveling in chance finds of furniture and objects from junk shops or flea markets. You could create this look yourself, hence the craze for learning to stipple, grain, and rag-roll paint. In spite of its eventual diffusion through interior style magazines, this eclecticism was often supported by good historical knowledge and an inquisitive eye for neglected beauty.

This Milan apartment is a good example of such a theatrical world of fantasy in a style that frankly acknowledges the pleasure of possessing books, pictures, and objects, and enjoys the accidental effects of draped textiles. The richness of color contributes to a feeling of warmth. While most modernist apartments seem ideal for summer, one feels drawn here by the prospect of comfort and entertainment on a winter evening when the outside world can be temporarily banished. The display of so many books promises more hours of productive self-instruction than the meager ration of a book or two and a magazine allowed in the typical minimalist apartment. And, even though there are a lot of objects in this interior, there is still plenty of space to hold a party.

The main living space is dramatically dominated by a wall hanging that is entirely modern in its abstraction and presents a mysterious touch in its glowing gold squares. At its foot, it is framed by a daybed,

THE APARTMENT CARRIES MANY HISTORICAL MEMORIES, BUT NEVER LETS THEM BECOME OPPRESSIVE. BOOKS AND OBJECTS ARE AN INVITATION TO LINGER AND ENJOY A RICH BACKGROUND OF CULTURE, WITH A FLAVOR AS MUCH FRENCH AS ITALIAN. SMALL OBJECTS ADD IMAGINATION AND INTEREST TO THE SHELVES OF LEARNED BOOKS

Above A narrow corridor links the main living spaces and the entrance, providing an attractive and welcoming vista of books and pictures lit by unseen windows. The piece of marble sculpture and the profiles of the Empire-style furniture enhance the space's feeling of classical elegance. Textured paint on the wall matches the leopard-skin print of the pillow cover to create a rich dappled effect in what might otherwise have been a dull and featureless passageway.

Right A detail of the study bookshelves, where leather-bound books mingle with miniature decorative objects, continuing the classical theme.

Far right Wooden models of staircases were originally used to teach stonemasons and architects, but they have a strong decorative appeal and add a pleasingly fantastical touch. The bookshelves' main uprights and horizontals have an effect of recessed panels on their faces; the whole is neatly fitted to allow space for the curtain.

Far left The unrestrained color of the bedroom provides a climax to the whole apartment, but the elements of the room are still disciplined by compositional symmetry and by the firm lines of the room itself. The simple folding tables are a practical device that allow this room to be used for work as well as pleasure.

Left Share your bathtime with the five orders of classical architecture, against a deep purple sky.

Below This robust bergère chair, upholstered with deep cushions, has the air of an experienced woman of the world, not averse to sharing confidences.

THEATRICAL BUT CONVENIENT FOR DAILY LIVING, THE APARTMENT'S SPACES ARE FLEXIBLE AND MULTI-FUNCTIONAL, WITH BOTH PUBLIC AND PRIVATE ROLES

a pleasing piece of nineteenth-century country classicism, matching in period the pedestal table in the center of the room. The corner windows are an unusual feature for a traditional apartment building, and give the room a single focus of light toward which one would be attracted in daytime.

This room links to the study, where the furniture is more formal although in the same style as before. The wooden models of staircase construction on the table have a strong decorative appeal, while the shelves are stocked not only with books but with curious objects to distract one's attention. As in the nineteenth century, the period which this apartment evokes, the specific functions of rooms are not too closely identified, and there is no absolute distinction between public and private space. One could set up a table for a meal in any of the rooms, and the bedroom could house a conversational group at a party, lacking the "off-limits" feel of many bedrooms. Even the bathroom serves as a gallery for architectural prints. The iron frame over the bed, originally intended for swathing with fabric to prevent drafts in unheated rooms, remains defiantly undraped and resembles a constructivist sculpture of the 1920s. The conjunction of rich red wallpaper and purple curtains, backed up by more red pillows, is a bold but successful choice of colors that gives the room a festive feeling as well as contributing to the apartment's feeling of comfort and pleasure.

THE SMOOTH MASCULINE EFFECT OF TRADITIONAL MATERIALS—LEATHER, CANVAS, FUR, AND FINE WOOD VENEERS—EVOKES A PREWAR LINER OR YACHT

Far left Simple colors and rich textures combine to create a luxurious feeling in this beautifully fitted-out 1930s apartment. The original dado paneling, incorporating radiator cases, provides a strong horizontal that is echoed in lines of the furniture. This room enjoys a flood of light, but the window blinds help to diffuse bright sunlight and provide a sense of privacy and restful ease.

Center left The folding leather safari chairs contrast with the solidity of the other furniture, while continuing the warm color scheme.

Left Furry furniture on four legs. One has a tail too.

Below The large leather rug provides an exotic and extravagant, but undeniably comfortable, touch.

LUXURY IN LEATHER
1930s COMFORT RECREATED

The subdued and masculine air of this 1930s Antwerp apartment is due in part to the unusual quality of the original interiors, which were almost unaltered when the designer Eric De Queker bought it from its first owner. The apartment building itself has an unusual pointed shiplike prow that gives the main living room four windows facing in different directions, overlooking a city park. Eric De Queker, who runs one of Belgium's best-known furniture and interior design companies, has created a balance between the sense of nature outside and the feeling of warmth and enclosure within.

The fine veneered wood finishes of the doors, built-in cabinets, and the wide arch that connects the two main parts of the living room set the tone for color and style, supported by the rich, golden wood flooring. The inner part of the living room, presumably originally intended to contain a substantial dining table, has a simple

beamed ceiling, reminiscent of the early modernist villas of the Austrian architect Adolf Loos, who used vestigial traditional details such as these to differentiate spaces and give them character. Here, the white-painted beams cast shadows and give the space perspective. The inner area is painted mushroom brown, while the view back from the far end of the room is framed by a bold gesture of black paint, setting the wooden frame of the archway into relief and creating a more mysterious feeling of light beyond in both directions. The bedroom, with wood paneling like that of a ship's cabin, is also painted to emphasize inward-looking comfort and offer a mood of contemplation, with a dark-blue ceiling suggestive of a night sky.

Within this simple but luxurious framework, Eric De Queker has carefully placed individual items of furniture that match the apartment's color and mood. These include the low-slung wood and leather safari chairs, an

Left The apartment benefits from two large interconnecting rooms, which house two sitting areas of contrasting mood and color that act as an ideal showcase for Eric De Queker's collection of furniture. The mirror-symmetry of the two seating units against the back wall establishes a formal composition of furniture that is centered on the solid pedestal of the low glass-topped table.

Right The lay light in the hall ceiling establishes a strong geometry for the space, but the walls are attractively mobile as they curve to narrow the space at each end. Behind this viewpoint are the kitchen and original servants' quarters.

Above The recess that houses the bed, in a wall that is built out to provide closet space, is an attractive original feature of the apartment.

Right The enlarged flower photograph is an unexpected but entirely appropriate way of bringing the bed recess to life. The large bed and bedside table continue the theme of solid cubic furniture that runs through the whole apartment. The bedside light is an original fixture from Eric De Queker Design.

Opposite In the bathroom, the original porcelain twin sink unit standing opposite the bathtub is entirely appropriate to the scale of the room. The white fur rug on the floor not only provides a welcome contrast of texture, but its irregular edges also offset the rigid grid of the tiled walls. The faucets are a miniature reflection of the larger unit. In a monumental bathroom like this, only a solid roll-top bathtub seems right.

NEW ITEMS OF LIGHTING MEAN THAT THE APARTMENT IS A
SHARP CONTEMPORARY MIXTURE, NOT AN INTERWAR PASTICHE

inspiration for the modern furniture of Marcel Breuer and Le Corbusier in the 1920s, even though they were designed to be conveniently portable in a canvas bag rather than with any conscious intention of being "modern." The line of all the seating is equally low, and includes a long sofa by Nathalie van Reeth and gray-flannel-covered seating by Jean de Mulder. These unusual materials—the coffee table is covered with brown fur and stands on a mat of black leather squares—demonstrate Eric De Queker's interest in texture as an aspect of design, something that usually works best, as here, within a limited color palette.

The broad hall is veneered in striped rosewood and recalls the great ocean liners of the Art Deco period. Here the lighting, furniture, and picture-hanging all bring attention down toward the floor, in preparation for the mood of the main rooms beyond. The bathroom is distinguished by its unusual double sink, a splendidly solid piece of interwar sanitaryware in an avocado color that matches the rest of the original fixtures. The fur rug takes the chill off the tiling and continues the tactile quality of the other rooms where it is most wanted.

Far left In the main living room, white and off-white textiles set the main color theme for a calm interior. The purple window seat adds variety and depth to the space. The large Doulton Acid Jug was a design favorite in the 1930s because of its simple, unselfconscious form and its usefulness for flower arrangements.

Left An Adam-style fireplace does not look out of place in this relaxed non-period assembly of furniture and objects. The brick-lined opening adds an English country element, contrasting with the smooth geometry of the picture hanging above.

Below This low level view of the tablescape shows how the casual-looking assembly of objects depends on a sense of visual structure.

MINIATURE PERFECTION
EVERYDAY HARMONY

The best interior design is impossible to reduce to a formula or describe as a style. Words and pictures can only go so far in conveying the quality of a room or an apartment. The personality of such spaces comes through a whole range of choices made on a day-to-day basis, rather than being enshrined in permanent visual form. Ann Boyd, the creator of this London apartment, is an experienced and successful designer who has worked for Ralph Lauren, and her work shares much with the developing sense of what is classic in fashion—something that is neither strictly traditional nor modern, but instead is an intuitive pathway between, with wide margins for personal choice on either side. When "classic" becomes a synonym for "static," then it shrivels and dies; it is necessary to be conversant with changing lifestyles and fashions, giving them a structured interpretation without being ruled by them.

DISCIPLINE AND POISE IN
THE UNDERLYING STRUCTURE
ALLOW THE EVIDENCE OF
LIVING TO ANIMATE THIS
APARTMENT'S ELEGANCE

Above A fake bamboo chair is one of the pieces
in the apartment that adds a touch of warmth
and personality.

Left The bedroom could hardly be more simple,
but shows the need for well-informed choices of
textiles and paint colors when decorating in an
understated style. The bed linen picks up light
and shade in an attractive modulation,
contrasting with the smoothness of the other
surfaces such as the headboard.

Right The "lived-in look" comes from the
evidence of ordinary life. The books look as if
they are there to read, not for show, while the
pieces of antique luggage act as a side table
and storage space combined. The comfortable
sofa, with its inviting pillows and reading lamp,
clearly welcomes visitors.

Above Lemons and polished pewter chime a color harmony in a minor key, in an apartment where no discordant colors are allowed to intrude.

Left A kitchen where everything is chosen to create a feeling of lightness and wellbeing, without any overstatement. The cane-backed chairs add a touch of French rusticity, which always activates the taste buds. The shutters modulate the light and provide a visually engaging form of privacy.

Right Casually piled Chinese ceramics introduce a strong blue note into the color palette.

Far right Ann Boyd made this picture from pieces of mother-of-pearl that originally belonged to an African necklace. Held on pins sticking through a linen backing, they cast shadows to track the path of the sun.

NO SLAVE TO CHANGING FASHION—A PALETTE OF BLUES AND YELLOWS PROVIDES ACCENTS OF ATTRACTION IN THIS COOL APARTMENT, BASED ON THE CLASSIC COLOR WHITE

Calm and space underlie the structure of this apartment overlooking the River Thames. It is not large, and the present arrangements have resulted from a process of elimination and simplification. Curtains are foresworn to gain maximum light, but glare is avoided by plantation shutters inside the window frames. The apartment is unified by use of the color white, but this is subtly interpreted and broken down into a variety of paint shades and fabric textures, blending in perfectly with the pale wood furniture. Even the pictures on the walls conform to this color regime, and the small number of objects that provide color accents do so as accessories, never taking control. The whole demonstrates the versatility and timelessness of white. The off-white carpet running through all the rooms except for the kitchen provides a unifying base for the seductively comfortable seating, convenient occasional tables, and few quirky gestures that prevent the apartment from being too impersonal.

THESE ROOMS ARE BIG ENOUGH TO HOUSE A CADILLAC
WITH FINS—A CONFIDENT ASSERTION OF SPACE THAT
SEEMS AN ESPECIALLY AMERICAN CHARACTERISTIC

Left This rough wooden African bench, carved from solid wood, acts as a sofa table, in proportion to one of a pair of 14-foot sofas that command the main living space.
Right A mysterious architectural photograph by Jim Casebeare hangs over the sofa. In the foreground is a 1940s swivel chair by the movie actor-turned-designer Billy Haines. The coffee tables display works of art, including a book ball by the artist Anne Hamilton, a paper sculpture made of the pages of a single book.

WIDE OPEN PLAN
CLASSIC AMERICAN STYLE

This spacious New York apartment reveals the discerning eye of its designer Steven Learner. It is modern in style, but with a historic and specifically American dimension in the choice of furniture that sets it apart from apartments furnished with modern classic pieces. The furniture is a mixture of carefully selected American designs from the 1930s and 1940s and newly made pieces specially adapted to the design of the space—notably the pair of 14-foot-long sofas that face each other from opposite ends of the 600-square-foot living room. These are a bold gesture of commitment to the apartment, since even by the spacious standards of New York, it is unlikely that they would fit anywhere else, but they are the making of the room, astonishing in their sheer size but perfectly comfortable and sociable. At one end, they form a sitting area with a pair of low-slung armchairs that recall the modernist Gerrit Rietveld's geometric red, blue, and yellow chair of 1919. These are, in fact, recent creations by Snook Studios, and just right for their context.

Above Details like this fruit bowl contribute to the conjunction of careful style and everyday living.

Left The southern end of the main room, where one of the 14-foot sofas lurks behind the door, contains neomodernist chairs by Snook Studios and a floor lamp made of sculptural wooden blocks. An off-white mat defines the sitting area and supports the restrained color scheme. A Richard Serra aquatint hangs on the wall behind.

Right above The apartment has ample space for the display of furniture and works of art, like this African chair and sculpture by Donald Judd.

Right below The family living room, with a generous sofa and charming table lamps. This room doubles as a guest bedroom.

In this main room, Learner has made subtle changes to the architectural form that help to make the scale comfortable. Baseboards were lowered and the door openings widened and given new architraves. The result preserves the basic vocabulary of the 1907 apartment building, but makes it a suitable setting not only for the furniture, but for a remarkable collection of contemporary art, some of which is displayed, in the manner of a gallery, in the large windowless central hallway, from which all the other rooms of the apartment can be reached. The inclusion of some pieces using neon lighting,

ART AND FURNITURE ALIKE EMPHASIZE INDIVIDUAL CHARACTER, BUT ARE BLENDED INTO A COHERENT SCHEME WITH A FLAVOR OF ITS OWN—CLASSIC AMERICAN STYLE WITH AFRICAN HIGHLIGHTS

one of which is by Dan Flavin, one of the best-known practitioners of this genre, helps them to double as a means of lighting the space. Between the windows, the absolute light of Flavin's neon tubes is contrasted with the inky darkness of an aquatint by the sculptor Richard Serra in which the printed surface comes close to reproducing the rusty steel surfaces for which his sculptures are famous.

This is a family apartment that is home to two small children, and one of the smaller rooms is set aside as a family living room with a television and a comfortable sofa. The consistency of the design does not let go here, however, and simple modern pieces of furniture are joined by a chair by the well-known American designer Robsjohn-Gibbings. Another room (pictured on page 144) is mysteriously sheathed in gray felt and serves as a dining room when required.

BARNETT NEWMAN

EDWARD RUSCHA

MAASA

The chairs are by Edward Warmley, but the table has been custom-made to raise and lower itself as required, serving equally as a coffee table or dining table.

This apartment is on a corner of the building, and the main bedroom gets the advantage of the double aspect. The bed is boldly placed against one of the windows and emphasized with a magnificent custom-made wooden headboard, left with a natural wavy finish on its upper edge. The use of massive wood is one of the distinguishing themes running through the furnishing of the apartment, notably in African pieces, such as the stool and coffee table in the main living room and the chair that stands beneath the wall-mounted Donald Judd sculpture in the hall. The roughness and weight of all these items prevents the apartment from becoming too ethereal in feeling.

THIS STYLISH APARTMENT HOUSES AN ART COLLECTION, YET ALSO WORKS AS A FAMILY HOME, WITH PLENTY OF SPACE FOR ACTION, AND EVEN A TELEVISION ROOM

The kitchen has the same solid but sparse feeling as the rest of the apartment, equally suggestive of the American mid-twentieth century that now inspires a high degree of nostalgia. The family dining area (pictured on page 114) has bright red upholstered bench seats such as one might find in an old-fashioned diner. The color and style of the tableware matches the 1940s modern feeling in many of the apartment's details. Stainless-steel cabinets and equipment complete this reassuringly heavyweight ensemble. In the relatively small bathroom the mood is lighter and more minimal, with a pale blue mosaic on floor and walls.

Despite its imposing art collection, the apartment has a festive feeling. Its spaciousness makes it ready to welcome a crowd of people, while its more intimate spaces make it a comfortable place for an evening *en famille*. This is the sort of city living that many people would like to achieve.

Left Use of space in the bedroom could have been awkward, with windows on two walls, but the problem is superbly solved by the wooden headboard, whose wavy silhouette adds unexpected charm. The way it extends on each side of the bed helps to show off the white tulip-style bed table and 1960s lamp. The dark wood floor is a good match for it.

Right above The simple bathroom is distinguished by its blue mosaic tiling. There is a subtle similarity between the butt-jointed mirror panels and the detailing of the handleless drawer fronts.
Right below The kitchen is practical and workmanlike, without frills but with a sense of visual consistency and style.

ECLECTIC
AND INDIVIDUAL

Left The Highpoint penthouse is entered through the door behind the pillar. Here the low ceiling provides an intimate sitting area around a fireplace with vertical pine boarding, one of many recreated features in this famous and unique space. Light comes mysteriously down onto the display shelf, where 1930s ceramics meet an African wood sculpture.

Right Emerging direct from the elevator, visitors remove their shoes by the bench, which is one of the surviving original features. Pine logs make a baffle, half concealing the view to the west until one sees it complete through the panoramic windows of the main room. The tile pattern runs through the main rooms.

CULTURAL CROSSROADS
PARADOX PAST AND PRESENT

To devotees of modern architecture in England, the penthouse at Highpoint II, the second of a pair of 1930s apartment buildings in north London, is a mythical, even a sacred space. The architect of the buildings, the mysterious and charismatic Russian Berthold Lubetkin, lived here from the time of their completion, shortly before World War II, until retiring to the country in the 1950s. The penthouse tested the boundaries of modern architecture, introducing layers of additional and contradictory meanings into what many people still think of as an over-functional, unpoetic style. The apartment's restoration has been continued by its present owners, who bought it in 1996 and have shown an inspired devotion to this space, rejoicing in their good fortune at being able to live here.

The Highpoint penthouse feels like London's rooftop. It did not need to fit into a structural grid like the apartments on the floors below, so Lubetkin gave the roof a curved profile, creating a high space in the center as well as a feeling of enclosure. The wind up here can make it seem like a storm at sea. In addition to smooth plaster on concrete, Lubetkin introduced a wall clapboarding of rough pine, evoking a log cabin in the wilderness. This shaggy quality was echoed in the furniture he designed for the penthouse.

Much of the interior has had to be restored, using the skill and knowledge of Lubetkin's biographer, the architect John Allan. The process began even before the present owners moved in. Thanks to their slow and meticulous restoration, original features of the interior are returning one by one. Notable among these, and perhaps the most eccentric gesture in a supposedly modern interior, is the use of hand-colored cutout sheets for Pollock's toy theaters as wallpaper on the wall between the kitchen and the original dining

LUBETKIN'S INDIVIDUAL MIXTURE OF ELEMENTS FROM 1938 HAS INSPIRED A GRADUAL RECONSTRUCTION OF HIS VISION, BUT IT IS A FLEXIBLE FORMULA THAT ALLOWS OTHER VOICES TO SPEAK. THE OWNERS SAY THAT LIVING HERE HAS CHANGED THEIR LIVES

Left Contemporary furniture by one of the joint owners of the apartment. "If you can't lift it, it's designed by me," he says. The diversity of style in the original design of the penthouse makes it receptive to objects of almost any character. The chunky forms relate well to the tile grid while contrasting with the other furniture nearby.

Above Berthold Lubetkin chose to decorate the outside of the kitchen wall with Pollock toy theater prints, a

form of Victorian folk art. The wall is now restored with authentic copies of the originals, full of soldiers, sailors, harlequins, and maidens in distress. Since the prints fit the walls exactly, he must have conceived the idea at an early stage.

Right The kitchen has been newly put in. The window is flanked by panels of glass brick, a popular material in the 1930s and one that contributes to Lubetkin's game of "now you see it, now you don't."

SUBLIME AND INTIMATE SPACES COMBINE TO CREATE A WORLD OF FANTASY AND CHARM

area. These Victorian popular prints were still available in the 1930s from Benjamin Pollock's shop in Hoxton, London. Staff at Pollock's Toy Museum, its successor, found the same sheets that Lubetkin had originally used. Next to them, the original shelf units have been recreated, with their deep red background color, found after scraping the wall, which complements the restored original blue of the ceiling.

The penthouse is not just a museum reconstruction, however, but reflects the taste of the owners, one of whom is a painter, the other a designer and maker of furniture. They claim that their understanding of visual style has been transformed by the experience of living here in a space that is continually revealing new subtleties of design.

Left The grand central space is sparsely furnished, giving a feeling of serenity. The windows command panoramas of London and give access to the roof terraces that run all around the apartment. A long travertine marble shelf runs beneath the windows.

Above left and right The bathroom has been recreated in its original position with tiles the color of an old architectural blueprint.
Right A work space with an Eames chair in a corner of the main room. The recreated bookshelves are just behind.

CASUAL CHARM
A COLLECTOR'S EYE

Objects can act like the words of a language. It is not like the sort of spoken and written language in which we hope to communicate exact meaning to each other, but still one in which meaning is produced by putting things side by side. The idea of the "amusing" object, which really means one that attracts attention by being placed deliberately out of context, would make an interesting study. Probably most people never feel the urge to disorganize the world in this way, seeing their possessions as strictly functional or at least uncorrupted by duplicity or ambiguity of meaning, but, as the ancient Greeks realized in their earliest rules for making works of art, it is strangeness that makes you think and feel emotion, not familiarity. "Amusing" objects may date back to the European taste for oriental exotica in the eighteenth century, when the Chinese were seen by distant Europeans as magical, wise, and also rather comical. Surrealism in the 1930s was probably responsible for the twentieth century's intermittent obsession with selecting the "wrong" things in a home, which for some people becomes almost a matter of honor and duty to an artistic ideal.

Left The use of a church pew as a room divider introduces the theme of pleasure in the ambiguity and dislocation of objects that runs through this apartment.

Above left The mixture of decorative textures in the floors, furniture, and in the picture to the right of the doorway gives interest and a kind of consistency to this foyer space, suggesting exotic and distant places seen through the medium of a fairground.

Above right The main sitting space, with its remarkable Art Nouveau-style center table.

Above Antique ceramic drawers for spices and dry goods are among many details that suggest a traditional Italian kitchen.

Left While the kitchen continues the theme of odd and unusual objects from the rest of the apartment, it has an airy lightness that provides a sense of wellbeing. The hanging light, adapted from an old kerosene lamp, is a particularly attractive piece, with its tendrillike brackets writhing up from the oil reservoir to the glass shade.

Right Old-fashioned kitchen equipment often has a strong sense of personality in its design. Even this refrigerator looks like a favorite aunt encamped behind the door. Appliances of this kind have enjoyed a nostalgic revival, and contemporary designers are now trying to give white goods more character.

Far right Italy has probably produced a greater variety of coffee-making equipment than any other country. Here a variety of styles are arrayed for display and use, joined by a sturdy juice extractor.

The English art writer Adrian Stokes once described artists as "psychical removal men," bringing people's mental furniture out onto the sidewalk, where it is displayed in all its oddity. Decorating with incongruity could be described as a reversal of this process, a kind of construction of a personal world through objects, reflecting the random and illogical aspects of life in a structured if always slightly unpredictable combination.

This Milan apartment, while apparently sedate and perfectly normal, with its background of white-painted walls, offers as varied a collection of objects as one

MEMORIES OF PAST TIMES CROWD THE KITCHEN AND PROMISE GOOD LIVING TO COME, BUT THEY ADD A SLIGHTLY DISTURBING TOUCH OF THE SURREAL. OLD-FASHIONED ITALIAN TERRAZZO FLOORS OFFER A NOSTALGIA OF THEIR OWN

might expect to find in that kind of small local museum that has not rationalized its holdings. It does not matter much whether they are valuable or intrinsically beautiful, since they have been assembled to provide a stimulus for the eye and the imagination as well as to serve the functions of living. The church pew that half divides the dining area from the living room is an object which, if seen in its proper place, would not be at all remarkable. Here it not only causes a tremor of recognition, more potent, undoubtedly, for those of good Catholic upbringing, but it reveals its strange and pleasing abstract shape, unlike any other piece of furniture from the normal household repertory. In its homey setting, it also provides three useful surfaces for putting things on as well as some additional seating. Here the white walls prevent the feeling from becoming too obsessive, while the variety of wooden furniture echoes the fine parquet flooring.

The hallway, with its typical Italian terrazzo floor sprinkled like the cocoa-powder dusting on a tiramisu, offers the encounter of a chair in richly painted folk-art baroque style with a wall cabinet whose lower doors sparkle with pieces of decorative colored glass like hard candy.

Left Speckled terrazzo continues into the bathroom floor and up the sides of the monumental bathtub. The huge mirror frame was surely never meant to grace such a humble setting, but it is both decorative and practical.

Right An elegant sleigh bed adds to the feeling of travel and adventure created by the artful disorder of the bedroom. At the same time, this is a perfectly practical arrangement, where the old suitcases can provide additional storage space.

Right and far right Books, shoes, and suitcases have begun to proliferate, as in a play by Eugene Ionesco. They create a miniature landscape on the floor, where the shoes inhabit striped beach cabanas and the suitcases dream of faraway adventures.

Below A simple chair is set off to advantage by the tiled wall that picks up a blurred shade of its curved back rails.

A TASTE FOR THE UNEXPECTED OBJECT, GADGET, OR
APPLIANCE KEEPS INTEREST ALIVE IN EVERY CORNER
OF THE APARTMENT AS LIFE FLOWS BY

The food and sweet-stuff metaphor continues with the picture
made of beans and grains. The oddest thing in the central
room is right in the middle: the pedestal of the table. Perhaps
its extended, tendrillike arm is meant to steady the
precarious-looking marble top, but it gives it a not-entirely
reassuring sense of being alive. It has a couple of young and
upwardly mobile relations in the two curly, iron fruit bowls.

This is an apartment where the kitchen continues the
decorative language of the other rooms, combining
practicality with oddity in the presence of the old meat-slicing
machine, the heavy weighing scales taken from an old grocery
store, and a robust coffee grinder. The curtainless windows
and the high white walls give a sense of freedom and release,
while traditional storage jars and spice drawers promise good
food to come. There is also a good central table, on well-
turned legs, which looks like an unambiguous place for a
traditional Italian family meal.

**MODERN SIMPLICITY AND THE ENGLISH COUNTRY-HOUSE LOOK
ARE JUDICIOUSLY COMBINED BY LIGHT, WHITE, AND INDOOR TREES**

Far left Light falls invitingly onto a long sofa beneath the sloping roof. The fine Chinese pot containing the indoor tree is one of several decorative elements in a space that is otherwise white.

Center left In an apartment where plants make a strong contribution, indoors and out, these cacti nestle comfortably on the bookshelves.

Left A series of literary classics by Milan publishers Einaudi forms a delightful color background to the main living space. Whoever chose these subtle colors might have dreamed of finding them displayed so invitingly as a complete library.

FOLIAGE IN THE SKY
A WHITER SHADE OF PALE

Walking along the narrow streets of Milan, one is frequently surprised by the sight of trees high up on the skyline, growing on the upper terraces of the apartment buildings and forming the most luxuriant roof gardens in Europe. This Milanese home is typical of the city's apartments in having well-planted roof terraces so gardenlike that for a moment you think they could be on terra firma. Here the trees and plants also come indoors, making their own structure in the space as well as providing decoration. Indoor plants are perhaps popular and widespread enough not to warrant any special comment, but the current trend of fashionable decoration is against such a lively expression of nature inside, preferring a tight geometrical structure. It seems a shame to deny the potential of plants, however, for they have practical as well as decorative advantages for interiors, bringing freshness to the air and a general feeling of wellbeing.

TREES INDOORS AND OUT ASSIST IN A PROCESS OF
ENJOYABLE DISLOCATION, WHERE SPACE EBBS AND
FLOWS AROUND SIMPLE FURNITURE

Here, the background of whiteness in paintwork and
upholstery fabrics makes an excellent foil for the two big
Ficus benjamina trees in the main living space. It is not
hard to imagine the different shadow patterns their leaves
could cast by day or night. This simple color scheme is
modified by well-chosen color accents, especially by the series
of paperback books ranged in the deep shelves beneath the
skylights. Other accents come from the blue glass jars on their
high shelf, which seem to chime with the hydrangea blooms.
The single touch of a pink carnation adds to this spectrum
where aggressive color is absent.

In this apartment objects come in families, not only the
trees and the books, but also the white Eero Saarinen tables.
These 1960s furniture classics have re-emerged in the current

Far left Trees and Eero Saarinen tables are grouped like families of objects. Behind the sofa is the dining table, with a row of chairs standing ready.

Center left A room divider storing glass tableware divides the kitchen from the main space without loss of light.

Left The dining area is slightly darker than the rest of the apartment, allowing a greater sense of intimacy. Its rear wall is dissolved by reflections, while the delicate bubble of the antique glass chemist's jar on the table brings an element of the past into well-judged alignment with modern living.

Above A corner of the roof terrace, well stocked with greenery in typical Milanese style.

revival of interest in that period. There is no conflict, however, between these modernist tokens of high technology and the sofas and chairs, which belong to a refined version of the English country-house look.

One of the main unifying factors is light—coming from the side and above, it is bounced off the reflective wooden floor, nowhere interrupted by carpets or rugs, and off the mirrors. The large one leaning against the dining area wall and the overmantel mirror both stand close to glass doors opening onto the roof terraces, thus setting up two different kinds of reflection in the vertical plane, while the white table tops add their own milky lakes. White gloss finishes on the woodwork complete this effect of maximum light, but the matt textiles prevent it from becoming excessive and provide a pleasing contrast.

The fireplace might come as a surprise in such an apartment, but its mannerist style, with its projecting shapes of white marble, suits the varied decorative language of the interior. Perhaps its aptness echoes the old alchemical division of the universe, for it adds fire to this microcosm of the elements of earth and air, amid pools of liquid light.

Above Details of an almost baroque richness pervade this more intimate sitting area. This view shows how different objects can act as screens, not only the painted folding screen itself, but the voile drapery and the shelf, which makes the opening more enclosed while still permitting a view through above.
Left A glimpse into the bathroom, which seems spacious despite its sloping ceiling. The towels are part of a series of blue objects whose careful placing helps to give the apartment a visual structure.

Right This realm of light and air is composed with subtle echoes of visual correspondence and rhythm, like the curvaceous duet between the bureau's front and the serpentine lintel of the fireplace. The 1960s table seems to come from an opposing culture of decoration to the bombé-fronted bureau, deeply upholstered white sofas, chairs in white covers, and the rough terra-cotta flowerpot, but a combination of careful control and a little spontaneity makes them a harmonious mix.

Left and below An accumulation of small decorative details makes Philippe Model's Paris apartment a place of varied visual enjoyment.

Right The classically proportioned rooms, leading from one another enfilade in the typical French plan, form a solid backbone along which changing and shifting arrangements of furniture and color are made. The painted areas of color are often the result of fashion shoots in particular corners of the apartment, but have become part of the signature of the space.

THE APARTMENT LENDS ITSELF ENTIRELY TO THEATRICALITY IN ITS ROLE AS AN EVER-CHANGING BACKGROUND TO WORK AND PLAY

MAD AS A HATTER
FASHION FUSION

A long time ago, "over the store" used to be the place where the shopkeeper lived, but it is now unusual for the rooms above small stores to have any connection with what goes on downstairs. This is a shame, because there are often unappreciated architectural riches to be discovered in older downtown buildings. In Paris, the versatile designer Philippe Model, who specializes in hats and shoes, but also designs furniture and tableware, keeps the rooms above his store as a mixture of workshop, apartment, entertaining suite, and background for photographing his creations.

Below left In this Regency-style room the mood is mid-eighteenth century, with some free improvisation. Pierre Griperay's sculpture, in front of the mirror, has curling lines that go with the rococo detailing of the paneling.

Below right Designing shoes is an important aspect of Philippe Model's work. Their presence adds a surreal touch to the rooms, combined here with a heavy nineteenth-century tasseled fringe.

Right A doorway filled with panes of mirror glass creates an illusion of endless space and subtly modulated colors. The harlequin patchwork pillow cover is shorthand for the decorative philosophy of the apartment.

Model is in love with the past in a theatrical way, drawing on a variety of inspirations in order to make new shapes, and experimenting with color.

Paris has always been a city of apartments, and traditionally the first floor contained the grandest rooms of the house, arranged to lead out of each other and changing from semi-public space to the more intimate rooms at the back. Philippe Model's building dates from the seventeenth century, with alterations in the eighteenth century. It reflects the serene self-confidence of French taste during this period in its simple well-proportioned paneling, lightly touched with rococo decoration, and tall windows.

There are few modern conveniences here, even discreetly hidden from view.

Below Daylight falling onto crumpled, romantically patterned floral bedding creates its own form of rococo in the scene set by this typically French painted bed, while the walls show ample evidence of experiments with paint.

Right The slightly uneven parquet flooring breaks up the light and provides a subtle raw umber background to the paint colors. Philippe Model likes to buy reproduction furniture rather than originals and then experiment with painting it, as he has done with the pieces seen here. This cabinet room shows the variety of spaces in the apartment.

Opposite A vivid color universe is created through the stained-glass panes of the internal window, the green paneling, and the rustic red chair. In the background, the tiled floor leads toward a distant bathroom containing a nineteenth-century zinc bathtub.

This is a romantic apartment, where the past comes to life, not in the manner of a museum with correct period items, but more as a stage set where feeling is more important than fact. The mirrors that seductively enlarge the space may indeed be modern, distressed on the back to give a more flattering broken reflection.

Paint colors often start in odd places, running in a vertical line to a point not quite halfway across a panel, or creating a cubist effect of dissolving planes. Paneling such as this, broken into planes of different colors, often occurs as a background in many of the majestic late paintings of Georges Braque. Textiles are draped from ceiling to floor, and a kitchen in the oldest part of the house, stripped back to its wooden frame, looks like the setting for a candlelit seventeenth-century scene.

LIKE SLEEPING BEAUTY KISSED BACK TO LIFE, THE APARTMENT WARMS TO ITS OWNER'S IMAGINATIVE ADVANCES IN A DANCE OF FLIRTATION IN WHICH SOMEONE ALWAYS SEEMS JUST TO HAVE LEFT THE ROOM

Even if not authentic, this style of treating an old building has many benefits. It avoids the danger of stripping away all the layers of the past in an effort to turn the clock back to an authenticity that can never really be recaptured, and may kill off the charm that has accumulated over centuries. Many people feel moved by the soft broken textures and the sense of hidden history that old houses acquire over time, but feel that for everyday life these oddities must be smoothed away. An interior like this is also a valid frame for creativity in the present, so that the building itself can be a sort of education, revealing secrets of its identity and personality over time to an attentive and imaginative owner. It also allows a creative interpenetration between past and present, and is an eye-opener as well as a delight for visitors. Philippe Model actually lives in another apartment in Paris; this one, apart from being a playground and studio, has introduced a wider circle of people to his design ideas. So many of them wanted to own copies of the items he made experimentally for his own use that he now sells a Philippe Model Maison line.

ELEMENTS

Color is always acknowledged to be a personal matter, since noone has been able to demonstrate that any of us see the same colors as other people. However, it is possible to learn about color by a process of experiment and study without losing one's sense of personal taste and judgment. Cleverly used, color can be not only a decorative feature, but a structural element—a visual divider of space—or a creator of atmosphere, making a room seem larger, warmer, or cooler. Home is a great place to use your newly developed appreciation of color, and the results can produce intense experiences.

The color of an interior is usually taken to mean the dominant color of paint or wallpaper on the walls. This is an area where decisions usually have to be made before the room is complete with its furniture and textiles. A trained designer or decorator will be able to hold the whole scheme in their mind's eye beforehand, but the less well-qualified apartment owner must take a few chances. There are several ways to gain an understanding of the effects of color in advance. Manufacturers' samples in small cans can be painted either directly onto the wall or onto a piece of board. The advantage of the latter method is that the sample can be tried out in different lighting conditions when it is moved around the room.

A style that was popular in the 1950s was to feature two colors in a room, perhaps with three walls the same and the fourth in a contrasting color. These kind of effects have had a revival in restaurants and other public spaces recently, and you can have hours of fun mixing and matching. If you get seriously interested in using color in your home, it is best to buy some artists' paints, in gouache or acrylic form, and make your own mixtures, which a paint retailer may be able to match. Some of the best color effects come from overlaying one color on another on the wall itself. This can be done by glazing over a base coat or by using a slightly transparent form of paint, such as distemper. You can also make your own paint mixtures when nothing from the manufacturers' color charts seems right. The addition of a small

Above The pale blue of this shower cubicle not only evokes water and the sea, but helps to give it a solid identity like that of a miniature building. Its horizontal lines, like the joints in stonework or stucco, and doorcase flanking the glass both suggest a built structure of importance.

Left A startling and bold application of a violet color to the two bookshelves flanking the doorway enforces a classical symmetry in this apartment, but indicates a sense of fun. The strong architectural patterning around the door frame is a good cue for this audacity, and touches of red, yellow, and blue in the background make a color picture in depth.

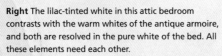

Right The lilac-tinted white in this attic bedroom contrasts with the warm whites of the antique armoire, and both are resolved in the pure white of the bed. All these elements need each other.

Far right This blue room in the Milan apartment featured on pages 50–57 is the one room in the apartment that does not follow the dominant whiteness of the rest. It offers a change of mood and a sense of privacy and retreat. The antique maps framed in the glazed doors contribute a warmer tone.

Below Not everyone will want to try the provisional look of Philippe Model's paint effects (see pages 102–107), but they help to show the endless variety of results that can come even from very similar paint colors. The traditional French paneling is excellent for modeling light and shade and for adding liveliness to the color surface.

COLOR IS A LANGUAGE WITH ITS OWN RULES, WHICH CAN BE LEARNED, BUT ARE HARD TO TRANSLATE INTO WORDS. IN SKILLED HANDS, IT CAN GIVE REAL CHARACTER AND INDIVIDUALITY TO A ROOM

amount of black, or of a complementary or contrasting color, gives a subtlety and depth that pure paint colors never quite achieve.

It is not surprising that so many white apartments feature in this book, as this is a color with which it is hard to go wrong. Remember, however, that there are many different kinds of white, which a skilled decorator may mix in one room, altering the warmth of tone to increase the sense of structure.

Color is also dependent on light, which changes through the day and through the seasons. In a single apartment, thought needs to be given to the orientation of the rooms and the warmth of the light that will enter them. Rooms that receive sun early in the day, or not at all, usually need some warming up with color, while rooms that benefit from afternoon or evening light will receive a redder light from the sun and need less artificial warmth. Night-time light conditions are equally important, but more easily controlled through electric lighting and its positioning.

We are currently in an era where color is beginning to make a comeback after a long spell of pure minimalist neutrals. However, if a space is small,

Left Most of the apartment designed by Eric De Queker is subdued in color (see pages 64–69). In this space, set apart from the main rooms, he has livened up a dark corner with strong red-painted shelves, backed by a wall of the same color, which flatters the objects of this varied collection.

Below The strong red benches in the kitchen of this New York apartment (see pages 76–81) give a cheerful feeling to an informal eating area, enhancing the 1940s character of the apartment with an unexpected and entirely appropriate suggestion of a highway diner.

Right A crowded, busy kitchen in the Milan apartment featured on pages 58–63. The "families" of matching objects provide a background of visual structure.

strong color is likely to make it seem smaller still, which may explain why most of the apartments featured in this book have color accents at most, giving the senses a jolt in contrast to more serene backgrounds.

The individual objects in a space offer the second way in which color can be used in a room. Much contemporary furnishing follows the trend of paint in neutrality and unassertiveness, but do try visiting historic houses. They are often eye-opening in their bold use of color in textiles and ceramics, especially compared to the cautious approach so often found today.

Pictures can provide valuable hints for color schemes, either by showing how two or more colors can go together in unusual and suggestive ways, or more specifically, when a particular picture is intended to hang in a room. It is possible to make the paint and textile colors a subtle complement to the picture and its color scheme, adding to the decorative unity in a room.

DIVIDERS

The design of a successful apartment depends on matching the available space to requirements that are not only functional but psychological. Space can be measured with a ruler, but its effect on the mind and feelings can be changed through design, and this is particularly important in apartment living, where the floor levels and ceiling heights are very often the same all the way through. One of the most effective ways of modulating space is through dividing rooms with partitions that are not the same as walls and doors, but allow a mixture of transparency and concealment. The result is a shift in mood from one space to another without the abrupt cutoff that comes from the solid enclosures of doors and walls.

French apartments of the eighteenth century, exemplified by Philippe Model's Parisian apartment (see pages 102–107), were planned with sequences of rooms that usually had two or three doors lined up with each other (an effect called an enfilade), allowing more distant views and the illusion of greater space. These doors probably stood open much of the time. Sliding doors (also known as pocket doors) became popular in the mid-nineteenth century because they allowed people to throw one room into another at will, whereas hinged doors of the same size would need a large space free of furniture in which they could swing. Pocket doors were usually positioned in the middle of a wall, and sometimes two sets opposite each other could allow three rooms to be joined together, creating a palatial space for entertaining. Because of their construction, they allowed a larger opening than would suit the proportions of a pair of conventional doors.

Apartment planning thus resisted the compartmentalization of living that featured in the Victorian period, and this fluidity of use in a relatively open space has remained a valued feature of apartment life. The simplest way to achieve an effect of half-closure is to remove the door and doorframe from an existing opening and plaster the opening.

The sliding door can retain its character as a door, or it can aspire to be a wall if it extends fully from floor to ceiling and fills the whole side

Above A simple door opening without a door helps to create a unity of space where there is no requirement for privacy. Having the same chairs on each side of this opening helps to link the two parts together.

Left This apartment is solidly furnished in a rather traditional way. The glazed sliding door in the foreground gives a choice between making the room beyond into a private library and study, or allowing it to be integrated with the rest of the apartment. Sliding doors are excellent space savers in apartments, needing no free wall on each side and, when open, creating the illusion of a generous space.

of a space. The New York apartment featured on pages 24–29 has a partition that thinks it is a wall, capable of closing off one end of the apartment as a guest suite. Concealing its identity to the last moment, the partition folds out like a two-leafed screen sliding in a track on the ceiling, leaving the floor unsullied by the evidence of any kind of lower track. The weight of its softly textured steel facings is held on two strong sets of piano hinges. This cannot be achieved cheaply or quickly, but it does relate to some of the most interesting ideas of the early Modern Movement in architecture, rethinking how people lived and allowing greater freedom of activity as well as a greater sense of togetherness.

A big change came when household servants disappeared and kitchens were upgraded to become important social hubs in the household. Older apartment buildings will probably still have a kitchen stuck somewhere at the back, with the least agreeable view and perhaps a long journey to the dining room. Where the kitchen is closer to the living spaces, it

Above The partition is cleverly designed to be flush with the wall surface when it is closed. The steel surface of the door contrasts with the stained wood—a feature of the apartment.
Left This beautifully constructed folding door in New York (see pages 24–29) makes a wall across the main passageway in the apartment, creating a separate guest suite when needed, but otherwise almost invisible, with only a ceiling track to hold it.

invites a variety of forms of division, so the person in the kitchen does not feel cut off from the rest of the apartment. The division may also include useful storage space, even those special drawers for flatware that pull out on both sides of the divider, allowing washed knives and forks to be fed in on the kitchen side and taken out when wanted on the dining-table side.

When a building is adapted, it may be necessary to keep parts of the structure for safety reasons. These do not always come where you want them, but when treated as room dividers, they can contribute to the character of the apartment. When these conditions do not apply, room dividers are often most effective when they stop short of the ceiling. This gives a top surface for displaying objects and helps to give the feeling of free-flowing space. It is also possible to lift dividers off the floor on slender supports, since the continuity of floor or ceiling surface is one of the best ways of giving the illusion of a more extensive space.

Far left A structural wall retained as a room divider between kitchen and living room in a relatively small New York apartment (see pages 42–47). The opening in the wall gives views to and from the kitchen.

Left The kitchen in this Milan apartment (see pages 96–101) has a close relationship with the main living space. The overhead shelf is practical and decorative, as well as framing the opening to a more domestic scale and breaking up the light from beyond.

Above In the same apartment, glass dishes are particularly well chosen for the openings in a screen between dining area and kitchen, catching the light and making a point of visual interest.

"The world is so full of a number of things/I think we should all be as happy as kings," says Robert Louis Stevenson in *A Child's Garden of Verses*. The world can seem too crowded with things, and however much one tries to keep control they invade one's living space.

Mastering storage in a living space, large or small, is one of the main ways in which design can contribute to everyday happiness. Apartments do not usually have the attics or basements of whole houses, so careful consideration of storage is necessary to avoid painful conflicts. One solution is to put it completely out of sight, perhaps in a small room like that in which Bluebeard kept his guilty secrets in the story, but pure storage of this kind, fine though it may be for the kind of items that companies and individuals can place in rented off-site units, is a waste of valuable space in an apartment.

The alternative is to integrate the storage into the living areas, so that one can still enjoy the vistas all through the kind of opened-up space that is one of the special advantages apartment structures, with a strong frame and few supporting columns, can usually offer. There is also an obvious benefit in having the things you want in different rooms. Many things can be stored in any room, and it may simply be easier to remember that they are in the second bedroom cabinet or in the space over the bathtub than trying to find them in a great mass of shelves and boxes all in the same place. However, opening up treasure boxes in a memory palace like this adds delight to the irksome subject of storage, an area that cries out for imagination and even a sense of humor. The multiplicity of little cupboard doors in the apartment on pages 30–35 shows how fantasy can come into play.

One of the most practical ways of providing storage is to thicken out walls and partitions so they can contain cupboards. These can be made accessible from both sides, which may mean from two rooms, and at the same time they can act as acoustic insulation. When it is undesirable actually to block off the space, the cupboards can be made into island units with openings cut through them. Sliding doors save a

Above This bookshelf on its sturdy wheels and runners is a neat way of adding storage capacity and at the same time making the process of searching the shelves an enjoyable activity in its own right. The contrast of light and dark shelving helps to make the sliding parts stand out.

Left Storage as a stage for drama. The ladder on its rail adds an enjoyable and practical way of reaching the high bookshelves, while the sliding doors below preserve the calm of a studious living space and allow a more relaxed regime of storage behind their forgiving concealment than open shelves would permit in the space.

Far left The use of the same unstained plywood for the bed, desk, and shelving gives this room the same unity of feeling as a ship's cabin, making storage unobtrusive.

Left A built-in closet, with its mirror door, is used to enlarge the space in this bedroom. The effect is continued with the mirrored trellis panel on its right.

Below A simple armoire in the style of a breakfront bookcase is less dominating in this room than a more conventional version with tall doors might be. The glazed doors with gathered curtains make an attractive pattern of reflected light.

lot of space, and sliding bookshelves are a refinement on this idea, not only saving space but inviting touch and use. The digital revolution has helped people who work at home to minimize the visual effect of papers and files, and it is now more common to find a laptop computer in a home than a bulkier desktop version, allowing greater flexibility in the allocation of working space.

Built-in storage saves space and contributes to the finished look of the apartment, but it can also be expensive to build properly. There are some shortcuts available from do-it-yourself stores, which can provide the internal structure for built-in units while leaving the outer surface coverings to be chosen separately or made to fit the space. Freestanding furniture is still an attractive alternative, where the piece concerned is the

STORAGE NEEDS TO BE WELL MADE AND PRACTICAL IF IT IS TO PROVIDE THE BEST VALUE IN LIMITED SPACE. SCALE AND COLOR MATTER AS WELL, BUT STORAGE CAN ALSO BE FUN

Far left This solidly built kitchen displays a mixture of practical and decorative pans and utensils. The central island provides some storage, in addition to the double-doored cabinet built into the corner recess.
Left and below Two views of the same kitchen in a New York apartment, where three small service rooms were combined into one generous kitchen, which succeeds in being the center of a family home. The tiled surfaces and sturdy equipment set the tone of old-fashioned practicality, while the overhead cabinets with steel doors add sparkle. Existing recesses in the wall are incorporated in the design.

right size and contributes to the character of the room, and both systems can of course be combined. The New York apartment featured on pages 42–47 combines built-in and freestanding items from the same designer. This creates a fascinating unity of effect, since there are almost no pieces in the apartment from any other source, and those that are used are carefully related to each other.

Kitchen storage offers a multitude of possibilities. While it can be organized so everything neatly disappears out of sight, as in the London apartment shown on pages 36–41, the attractive nature of kitchen utensils encourages many people to put them on display, even making them something of an antique collection (see pages 90–95). The kitchens shown here make the most of display, but a lot of thought has gone into the provision of good cabinets and drawers, leaving space for the display items to offset the heavy-industrial catering look often favored in contemporary kitchens.

Lighting is important: consider the amount of our lives we spend under artificial light. Until recent years, the choice of available lighting appliances was disappointingly small, given the length of time since electricity was first used and the enormous range of possibilities that it offers. Now the situation has improved as some of the classic twentieth-century lighting designs are more readily available, and new ideas and shapes are appearing in stores and the catalogs of specialized suppliers. It should now be possible to find items that express personal taste and contribute positively to the character of an interior.

Some people would argue that a light fixture should be as unobtrusive as possible, since its function is only to throw light on other things and not to draw attention to itself. This is not so easy to achieve in practice, as a bulb and shade necessarily take up space and it is hard not to see them. The best light fixtures combine practicality with a pleasing and interesting visual form that looks good even when it is not switched on. Nonetheless, the quality of light that comes from a particular source is a crucial consideration, and one which is hard to estimate accurately when you are shopping.

The job of designing lighting for an apartment only differs from that of any other space in the need for a coherent treatment that will make the space seem larger and avoid a feeling of clutter. Interior decorators usually make the distinction between background lighting and task lighting, the latter including most of the smaller movable lights. In reality, the difference has become blurred, and most lights are called on to perform both roles. The central overhead fixture is still the standard equipment for background lighting, but it is hard to make this rather harsh light feel part of a comfortable room. The closer to the floor the lighting is, the more it creates a feeling of calm and increases the sense of space. A flexible combination of floor and table lights may perform both the functions of background and task lighting. Instead of relying on a central light that switches on from the door, use wall sockets and switches, to which any light fixture can be connected.

Above A simple, low-level light in the Highpoint penthouse (see pages 84–89), with the warm quality of candlelight. Its wooden base is well matched both to the wood of the table on which it stands and the wooden paneling on the wall behind.
Left In the Antwerp dining room designed by Eric De Queker (see pages 64–69), the hanging center light has the delicate subtlety of a sculpture by Naum Gabo, making an object that would attract attention under any conditions.

Below left An overhead light for a dining table is carefully devised to blend almost invisibly into the darkness, while providing a well-focused light for eating and conversation that could be supplemented by candles on the table. The circular openings echo the holes in the chair backs and the circular table base.

Below center Some light fixtures illuminate entirely. This example has a simple but satisfying geometric shape based on squares and cubes.

Below right Lighting with attitude. This tripod floor lamp in the Paris apartment shown on pages 30–35 has a strong personality, suggesting a piece of sculpture welded from the products of an industrial junkyard. It is positioned so that much of its light is reflected from the wall, rather than dazzling one's eyes when moving past it.

Decisions about lighting always need to be made at an early stage, even if they only involve some concealed wiring for wall lights, but it is possible to go much further than this. There has been a revival in the kind of concealed lighting whose origins go back to the 1920s, when architects and designers first began to respond to electric light by incorporating it into the design of their interiors. Suddenly night became a time of poetry and wonder. Spotlight tracks, popular in the 1960s, added a greater flexibility in positioning, but never achieved the same elegance as concealed lighting. Built-in lighting involves a sense of commitment that many people now seem willing to offer to their living spaces, and it has become even more possible with the arrival of low-energy and small-scale bulbs and tubes. These can be concealed in narrow troughs built into the wall, or on the underside of shelving, and controlled with dimmers to give varied effects of background lighting with no visible fixtures. Lights can also be placed behind or beneath panels of obscured glass so they shine through the panels, providing glamour and mystery as well as saving space.

Candles have enjoyed a recent revival, and their warm glow and intimacy, on a table, a shelf, or a window ledge, cannot be rivaled by electricity. Votive candles are good for the table, clustered on a silver plate, since they do not block the view of the person opposite, as candles are apt to do. Not surprisingly, candles have always been popular in Scandinavia, where the winters are long and dark, and these countries have developed some of the best modern design for homes. Candles are not just reminders of a romantic past; the choice of candleholders and shapes now available includes many modern enough for any contemporary apartment.

Examples on these pages demonstrate a wide range of styles, each adapted to its context. A light fixture can contribute something positive to a room when it has been chosen to express the personality of the owner and the character of the apartment. It is better to be guided by a combination of what will work practically, providing the right kind of light in the right place; what goes with the decorative theme of the apartment; and what is surprising and unusual. There is no need for lighting to be dull or predictable.

Below left Simple light fixtures for a traditional look, with a hall lantern based on good eighteenth-century models, and a wall fixture in a similar style. The throw of light up to the ceiling is a bonus.

Below center A traditional-style electric chandelier with a matching plaster ceiling molding. The value of such fixtures is as much in the way they define the centrality of a classical room as in the quality of light that they provide. Sometimes a room demands a gesture of this kind, for a central molding without a light fixture tends to look barren.

Below right A table light that forms part of a group of still-life objects on a side table as well as providing an ample but regulated source of light.

Floor coverings can be a great way to pull a decorative scheme together and make the most of a small space. The modern preference for natural, hard-surfaced materials can be seen in nearly all the apartments in this book, and very few have much carpeting. This preference for hard surfaces is also found in restaurants and stores, and crosses the boundary between traditional and modern styles. At the same time, more and more people prefer to remove their shoes indoors, saving their flooring from the transfer of outdoor dirt while inviting their feet to have a more sensual engagement with the floor. This is the rule at the Highpoint penthouse. A wooden bench was placed by the lift entrance when the apartment was designed in 1938 and now serves to seat guests while they remove their shoes.

Wood is currently the most popular material for flooring, and it can often be found already existing in many apartments, either in the form of simple straight boarding, in herringbone blocks, or in more elaborate patterns of parquet. One advantage of wood over other materials is that it tends to improve with age and use, provided that no disasters occur. The grain will be revealed by general wear and tear so it catches the light, and any irregularities that exist will be absorbed into the general patina. The first rule of apartment flooring is therefore to see what floors there already are and whether the general decorative concept will work with them. This is commonsense and economy, but also a way of paying tribute to the character of the building. Existing terrazzo and tile finishes in kitchens and bathrooms contribute to the character of several of the apartments in this book, notably those in older buildings in European cities. New Yorkers are often sentimentally attached to their interwar apartment bathrooms, tiled from floor to ceiling and over the floor, with a built-in medicine cabinet over the bathroom sink, and renovate them with loving care. It is usually possible to repair small broken sections unobtrusively.

If you decide to create a completely new floor, the present trend is for uniformity throughout, which contributes to the feeling of space

Above Furniture can stand four-square on the floor, or, like this curved laminated stool, it can touch down lightly on a limited contact area. Details of this kind can help to bring attention down to the floor level, making the floorboards an object of attention in their own right.

Left The value of a good floor as a unifying design device can be seen in this New York apartment, with a dining area to the side of a generous hallway, extending into a main living room. The reflections on the polished wood surface show how effective this choice of flooring is for increasing the natural light in an apartment.

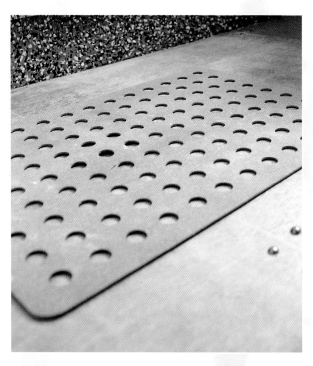

Opposite top left Traditional Italian terrazzo flooring is a nostalgic reminder of older times and well worth preserving. The different varieties are suggestive of different grades of Italian salami— some with a coarse grain, like this example; others, more finely processed.
Opposite top right Terrazzo with a closer grain in a bathroom. The colors of these floorings are often very attractive in their own right.
Opposite bottom left The stone flooring in this apartment (featured on pages 24–29) makes a luxurious contribution to the calm austerity of all the rooms, providing a warm tone that goes well with wooden furniture.
Opposite bottom right A checkered tile floor in the kitchen of the Paris apartment on pages 30–35, dating from the original design of the apartment and still going strong. The reflection in the steel bin is a bonus.
Left This kitchen floor in Milan (see pages 90–95) has the scattered, random quality of old terrazzo that seems to go with good traditional Italian housekeeping and home cooking.

and allows different room functions to be reallocated over a number of years. A durable and beautiful material like wood adds to the initial cost, but is a worthwhile investment, at least until fashion rediscovers linoleum. Stone, as seen in the New York apartment on pages 24–29, is less likely to be an option for most people, but gives a great architectural quality to the space.

Carpeting seems appropriate, however, for the bedroom in the New York apartment which is consciously trying to recreate a feeling of the 1960s and 1970s, when any other alternative would have been considered rather old-fashioned (see pages 42–47). A compromise between the comfort that carpets certainly provide and the present fashion for hard surfaces can be achieved in the form of squares of

FLOORS CONTRIBUTE TO THE MOOD OF A SPACE. HARD MATERIALS ARE AUTHENTIC, HARD-WEARING, AND GOOD AT REFLECTING LIGHT

Background picture this page The leather mat in the Antwerp apartment on pages 64–69 is an unusual but practical flooring material, being proof against spills of food or drink. The parquet has a pattern of its own with dark wood inlays.

Left Herringbone parquet usually has squared ends, but these pieces with mitered joints provide a satisfying visual pattern of chevrons in Philippe Model's apartment (see pages 102–107). The shoes show how objects on the floor can attract attention to this important level, which may otherwise go unappreciated.

Right Broad floorboards rule in early twenty-first century flooring. In the background, a glimpse of matting gives a clue to the space of the room beyond extending to the right. Baseboard details are an important complement to flooring. Here the reduction of the baseboard to a thin strip, of the same tone as the floor, helps to make the junction between floor and walls geometrically crisp, enforcing the solid geometry of the walls.

carpet laid on certain areas of floor to create warmth and give sound insulation. The current preference is for these to be unpatterned, and usually light in color. It is now almost a convention to leave a border of plain floor around the edge, which is something the eye seems to need in order not to "read" the underlying floor surface as a continuous whole.

There has been a revival in the design and making of large, abstract-patterned rugs, which help to focus the floor space around a sitting area or enliven a dark hall with color. The rugs in the Highpoint penthouse, seen on pages 84 and 88, are careful recreations of the originals—plain white but with a beautiful close pile, and intriguingly stitched together so the geometry of the three pieces contributes to the dynamics of the space. The Milan apartment shown on pages 50–57 has a more traditional-patterned rug, that works well in the context of a rather classical space. Even during the current trend for exposed surfaces, it is worth recalling the beauty of traditional rugs. They do not have to be laid on the floor, but can be hung on walls or used as table coverings.

SOURCE DIRECTORY

GENERAL STORES

ABC Carpet & Home
777 South Congress
Delray Beach, FL
For a store near you, call
(561) 279-7777
www.abchome.com

Bloomingdales
1000 Third Avenue
New York, NY 10022
(212) 705 2000
www.bloomingdales.com

The Conran Shop
407 East 59th Street
New York, NY 10022
(212) 755 9079
www.conran.com

Crate & Barrel
1860 West Jefferson Avenue
Naperville, IL 60540
For a retailer near you, call (800)
927-9202
www.crateandbarrel.com

IKEA
Potomac Mills Mall
2700 Potomac Circle
Suite 888
Woodbridge, VA 22192
For a store near you, call
(800) 254-IKEA
www.ikea.com

Neiman Marcus
For a store near you, call
(888) 888 4757
For mail order, call
(800) 825 8000
www.neimanmarcus.com

Pottery Barn
P.O. Box 7044
San Francisco
CA 94120-7044
For a store near you, call
(800) 922-9934

FURNITURE

Antiques Ltd.
Suite 1626, World Trade Center
Chicago, IL 60654
(312) 644-6530
www.antiquesltdchicago.com
One-of-a-kind pieces.

Dana Robes
Route 4-A
Lower Shaker Village
Enfield, NH 03748
For a retailer near you, call (800)
722-5036
www.danarobes.com
Shaker-style furniture.

The Federalist
Greenwich, CT
(203) 625-4727
Early 19th-century Federal-
period American furniture.

Maine Cottage Furniture
P.O. Box 935
Yarmouth, ME 04096
(207) 846-1430
www.mainecottage.com
Maple, birch, and cherry veneer
furniture.

McGuire
1201 Bryant Street
San Francisco, CA 94103
(415) 626-1414
www.mcguirefurniture.com
Rattan, cane, teak, bamboo, and
hardwood furniture.

Montis
Hendersonville, NC
(919) 942-1608
www.montis.nl
Leather and metal furniture.

George Smith LA
142 North Robertson Blvd.
Los Angeles, CA 90048
(310) 360-0880
www.georgesmith.com
English sofas and chairs.

Wilkening Fireplace
9608 State 371 NW
Walker, MN 56484
For a retailer near you, call
(800) 367-7976
Fireplaces, wood stoves,
screens, and enclosures.

COLOR

Benjamin Moore & Co.
51 Chestnut Ridge Road
Montvale, NJ 07645
For a retailer near you, call
(800) 344-0400
www.benajminmoore.com
Paint specialists.

Finnuren & Haley Inc.
901 Washington Street
Conshohocken, PA 19428
(800) 843-9800
Manufacturer of The American
Collection of historic colors.

Janovic
30–35 Thomson Avenue
Long Island City, NY 11101
For a retailer near you, call
(800) 772-4381
www.janovic.com

Old Fashioned Milk Paint Co.
436 Main Street
P.O. Box 222
Groton, MA 01450
(978) 448-6336
www.milkpaint.com

Martin Senour Paints
101 Prospect Avenue
Cleveland, OH 44115
(800) 542-8468

Wagstaff Tile
3720-C Alliance Drive
Greensboro, NC 27407
(336) 292-4993
www.wagstaff-tile.com
Handpainted ceramic tiles and
tumbled marble mosaic borders.

FLOORING

Aged Woods Inc.
2331 East Market Street
York, PA 17402
(800) 233-9307
Antique heart pine, hickory, ash,
and other unusual flooring.

Bangkok International
4562 Worth Street
Philadelphia, PA 19124
(215) 537-5800
Hardwood flooring.

The Burruss Co.
P.O. Box 6
Brookneal, VA 24528
(800) 334-2495
Oak, pine, maple, ash, walnut,
and cherry floors.

Congoleum
Department C, P.O. Box 3127
Mercerville, NJ 08619-0127
For a retailer near you, call (800)
274-3266
www.congoleum.com
Sheet vinyl, vinyl tiles, and wood
laminate floors.

Country Floors Inc.
8735 Melrose Avenue
Los Angeles, CA 90069
For a store near you, call
(310) 657-0510
www.countryfloors.com
Handcrafted, decorative floors.

Claremont Rug Co.
6087 Claremont Avenue
Oakland, CA 94618
(800) 441-1332
Antique art carpets.

Rug Oasis
115 West Avenue
Kannapolis, NC 28081
(800) 524-6902
Large selection of Karastan
carpets and other brands.

LIGHTING

Altamira Lighting
79 Joyce Street
Warren, RI 02885
(401) 245-7676
Contemporary table and floor
lamps.

American Period Lighting Inc.
3004 Columbia Avenue
Lancaster, PA 17603
(717) 392-5649
Handcrafted fixtures.

Electrics Lighting and Design
530 West Francisco, Suite 8
San Rafeal, CA 94901
(415) 258-9996

Home Depot
2455 Paces Ferry Road
Atlanta, GA 30339
For a store near you, call
(800) 430-3376

The Tin Bin
20 Valley Road
Neffaville, PA 17601
(717) 569-6210
Indoor- and outdoor-use lamps.

Top Brass
3502 Parkdale Avenue
Baltimore, MD 21211
(800) 359-4135
Antique, reproduction, and
contemporary lamps.

PICTURE CREDITS

Key: t = top, b = below, l = left, r = right, c = center

Front endpaper An apartment in Milan designed by Daniela Micol Wajskol, Interior Designer; 1 Bob & Maureen Macris' apartment on Fifth Avenue in New York designed by Sage Wimer Coombe Architects; 2 & 3 Apartment in Antwerp designed by Claire Bataille & Paul ibens; 4 tl An apartment in London designed by Jo Hagan of Use Architects; 4 tr An apartment in New York designed by Gabellini Associates; 4 b Mark Weinstein's apartment in New York designed by Lloyd Schwan; 5 t The London apartment of the Sheppard Day Design Partnership; 5 bl An apartment in Milan designed by Daniela Micol Wajskol, Interior Designer; 5 br Sig.ra Venturini's apartment in Milan; 9 l inset Paul Raftery/Arcaid; 9 c inset The Architects' Journal; 9 r inset Paul Raftery/Arcaid; 10 Paul Raftery/Arcaid; 11 t Sir John Summerson/Architectural Association; 11 bl Andrew Higgott/Architectural Association; 11 br Victoria Boyarsky/Architectural Association; 12 b the Maison Clarté in Geneva, 1930, designed by Le Corbusier, picture courtesy of the Fondation Le Corbusier in Paris; 12 r C. Hanbury/Architectural Association; 13 RIBA library photographs collection; 14 t Edifice/Darly; 14 b F.R.

Yerbury/Architectural Association; 15 Dennis Wheatley/Architectural Association; 16 tl The Architects' Journal; 16 tr Valerie Bennett/Architectural Association; 16 b Sir Denys Lasdun; 17 Valerie Bennett/Architectural Association; 19 tl Eric Lyons Cunningham Metcalfe; 19 tr Peter Blundell-Jones; 19 bl Paul Raftery/Arcaid; 19 br Rene Burri/Magnum Photos; 20–21 main Sig.ra Venturini's apartment in Milan; 20 inset l Ou Baholyodhin & Erez Yardeni's Penthouse, Highpoint, London; 20 inset c Mark Weinstein's apartment in New York designed by Lloyd Schwan; 20 inset r An apartment in Milan designed by Daniela Micol Wajskol, Interior Designer; 22–29 An apartment in New York designed by Gabellini Associates; 30–35 François Muracciole's apartment in Paris; 36–41 An apartment in London designed by Jo Hagan of Use Architects; 42–47 Mark Weinstein's apartment in New York designed by Lloyd Schwan; 48–57 An apartment in Milan designed by Daniela Micol Wajskol, Interior Designer; 48 Chinese rug from Alberto Levy Gallery, Milan. Round table and screen from L'oro dei Farlocchi, Milan. Bronze lamp from Polenghi e Maffei Antiquari, Milan; 50 Prints from Cristina Ballini Antiquario, Milan; 51 Picture above mantelpiece from L'oro dei Farlocchi, Milan; 52 l Chaise longue

from L'oro dei Farlocchi, Milan; 53 l Chairs from Cristina Bellini Antiquario, Milan; 55 l Wall-sconces from Carati, Milan. Wooden towel-rail from L'Utile e il Dilettevole, Milan; 55 r Plant holders from Tea Rose, Milan; 57 Kitchen table and chairs from Polenghi Antiquario, Milan; 58–63 An apartment in Milan designed by Nicoletta Marazza; 64–69 Eric De Queker's apartment in Antwerp; 70–75 Interior Designer Ann Boyd's own apartment in London; 76–81 An apartment in New York designed by Steven Learner; 82–89 Ou Baholyodhin & Erez Yardeni's Penthouse, Highpoint, London; 90–95 Gentucca Bini's apartment in Milan; 96–101 Sig.ra Venturini's apartment in Milan; 102–107 Philippe Model's apartment in Paris; 108–109 main Apartment in Antwerp designed by Claire Bataille & Paul ibens; 110, 111 & 112 t The London apartment of the Sheppard Day Design Partnership; 112 b Philippe Model's apartment in Paris; 113 An apartment in Milan designed by Daniela Micol Wajskol, Interior Designer; 114 t Eric De Queker's apartment in Antwerp; 114 b An apartment in New York designed by Steven Learner; 115 An apartment in Milan designed by Nicoletta Marazza; 116 Lisa & Richard Frisch's apartment in New York designed by Patricia Seidman of Mullman Seidman Architects,

interior decoration by Mariette Himes Gomez; 117 Apartment in Antwerp designed by Claire Bataille & Paul ibens; 118–119 & 119 An apartment in New York designed by Gabellini Associates; 120–121 Mark Weinstein's apartment in New York designed by Lloyd Schwan; 121 l Sig.ra Venturini's apartment in Milan; 122 Apartment in Antwerp designed by Claire Bataille & Paul ibens; 123 David Mullman's apartment in New York designed by Mullman Seidman Architects; 124 Bob & Maureen Macris' apartment on Fifth Avenue in New York designed by Sage Wimer Coombe Architects; 125 t The London apartment of the Sheppard Day Design Partnership; 125 b Lisa & Richard Frisch's apartment in New York designed by Patricia Seidman of Mullman Seidman Architects; 126 The London apartment of the Sheppard Day Design Partnership; 127 t & b David Mullman's apartment in New York designed by Mullman Seidman Architects; 128 Eric De Queker's apartment in Antwerp; 130 l Apartment in Antwerp designed by Claire Bataille & Paul ibens; 130 r François Muracciole's apartment in Paris; 131 l An apartment in Milan designed by Daniela Micol Wajskol, Interior Designer; 131 r An apartment in New York designed by Steven Learner; 132 David Mullman's apartment in New York designed by Mullman Seidman Architects; 136 Philippe Model's apartment in Paris; 137 Apartment in Antwerp designed by Claire Bataille & Paul ibens; 144 An apartment in New York designed by Steven Learner; Back endpaper Apartment in Antwerp designed by Claire Bataille & Paul ibens.

ARCHITECTS & DESIGNERS WHOSE WORK IS FEATURED IN THIS BOOK:

Ou Baholyodhin Studio
1st floor
12 Greatorex Street
London E1 5NF
t. +44 20 7426 0666
f. +44 20 7426 0330
e. oub@globalnet.co.uk
w. ou-b.com
Pages: 20 inset l, 82–89

Claire Bataille & Paul ibens
Vekestraat 13 bus 14
2000 Antwerp
t. +32 3 231 3593
f. +32 3 213 8639
e. bataille.ibens@planetinternet.be
Pages: 2, 3, 108–109, 117, 122, 130 l, 137, back endpaper

Ann Boyd Design Ltd.
33 Elystan Place
London SW3 3NT
Pages: 70–75

Eric De Queker
DQ – Design In Motion
Koninklijkelaan 44
2600 Bercham
Belgium
Pages: 64–69, 114 t, 128

Gabellini Associates
Michael Gabellini AIA,
Principal Designer
Dan Garbowit AIA,
Managing Principal
Ralph Bellandi, Sal Tranchina,
Jonathan Knowles AIA,
Project Architects
Stephanie Kim, Lisa Monteleone,
Tom Vandenbout, Project Team
665 Broadway, Suite 706
New York, NY 10012
USA
t. 212 388 1700
f. 212 388 1808
Pages: 4 tr, 22–29, 118–119, 119

Mariette Himes Gomez Associates, Inc.
Interior Decoration
504–506, East 74th Street
New York, NY 10021
USA
t. 212 288 6856
f. 212 288 1590
e. gomezny@ibm.net
Pages: 116

Steven Learner Studio
307, Seventh Avenue
New York, NY 10001
USA
t. 212 741 8583
f. 212 741 2180
w. stevenlearnerstudio.com
Pages: 76–81, 114 b, 131 r, 144

Nicoletta Marazza
Via G. Morone, 8
20121 Milan
Italy
t./f. +39 2 7601 4482
Pages: 58–63, 115

Philippe Model
Decoration, Home Furnishing & Coverings
33 Place du Marché St. Honoré
75001 Paris
t. +33 1 4296 8902
102–107, 112 b, 136

Mullman Seidman Architects
443, Greenwich Street
New York, NY 10013
USA
t. 212 431 0770
f. 212 431 0770
e. mullseid@monmouth.com
Pages: 116, 123, 125 b, 127 t & b, 132

François Muracciole
Architect
54, rue de Montreuil
75011 Paris
t. +33 1 43 71 33 03
e. francois.muracciole@libertysurf.fr
Pages: 30–35, 130 r

Sage Wimer Coombe Architects
480 Canal Street, Room 1002
New York, New York 10013
USA
t. 212 226 9600
Pages: 1, 124

Lloyd Schwan/Design
195 Chrystie Street, # 908
New York, NY 10002
USA
t. 212 375 0858
f. 212 375 0887
e. lloydschwan@earthlink.net
Pages: 4 b, 20 inset c, 42–47, 120–121

Sheppard Day Design
t. +44 20 7821 2002
Pages: 5 t, 110,111,112 t, 125 t, 126

USE Architects
11, Northburgh Street
London, EC1V 0AH
t. +44 20 7251 5559
f. +44 20 7253 5558
e. use.arch@virgin.net
Pages: 4 tl, 36–41

Erez Yardeni Studio
Function – 1st floor
12 Greatorex Street
London E1 5NF
t. +44 20 7426 0666
f. +44 20 7426 0330
Pages: 20 inset l, 82–89

INDEX

Figures in *italics* refer to captions.

142

ACKNOWLEDGMENTS

I am very grateful to the apartment owners who have allowed their homes to be included in this book, and entertained me on visits. The editorial staff of Ryland Peters and Small have been helpful and supportive at all times, and we are jointly grateful to the Architectural Association Slide Library, Andrew Mead of the Architectural Press Photo Archive, Sir Denys Lasdun, Ivor Cunningham, and Professor Peter Blundell-Jones for helping to supply photographs for the introduction.